NIGHT SWEATS

an unexpected pregnancy

Laura Crossett

Iowa City, Iowa
2013

Library Society of the World
Cataloging-in-Publication Data

Crossett, Laura.
Night sweats : an unexpected pregnancy / Laura Crossett.

    ISBN 978-1-304-00553-3

1. Crossett, Laura—Confessions 2. Pregnant women—Mental health
3. Christian biography—United States 4. Pregnancy, Unplanned—United
States 5. Wayward spinsters—Iowa—Iowa City 6. Intrauterine contracep-
tives—FAIL I. Title
      618.2—dc23
      RG525.C951 2012

for Peter

and in memory of my grandmother,
Joan Louise Hillmer Wallace
1923-2012

#260

I'm Nobody! Who are you?
Are you—Nobody—too?
Then there's a pair of us?
Don't tell! they'd advertise—you know!

How dreary—to be—Somebody!
How public—like a Frog—
To tell one's name—the livelong June—
To an admiring Bog!

Emily Dickinson

And these are the thoughts I was left with: that
romance is stupid and sometimes worth it; that
fellowship is risky and always worth it; that I
am ridiculous, and that I am not.

Anne Lamott,
from *Hard Laughter*

CONTENTS

AUTHOR'S NOTE

This is an account of one single woman's pregnancy. It is customary, in such narratives, for the father to be an absence and sometimes a villain. The author would urge the reader to consider that this is merely her story. The father has his own story, whether or not he chooses to tell it, and it should be respected.

The following pages were largely drafted as they are dated, initially as a series of posts on a private blog written for a small group of friends. Many were revised for this book, and a few were added later to provide more narrative cohesion.

PROLOGUE

Two weeks ago I killed my cat. Well, technically, the vet did it, and it's not called killing, it's called *euthanasia* or *putting down* or, most euphemistically, *putting to sleep*. I did this because he was old and sick. He weighed only 4.6 pounds, down from his eight-pound prime. He had an infection in both eyes and one paw. He was almost completely dehydrated. *Shrunken* is how the vet described him. He gave him only another twenty-four hours to live but then said he was such a tough cat he might hang on for another week, getting weaker and weaker. Everyone at the office was amazed he could still stand. I told them that the day before he had jumped on my bed. Twice. But I killed him, or I let him be killed, and then I buried him in the backyard, with the help of a friend who is the father of my baby but not my partner. It was dark by the time I got started, and I was digging by the light of a railroad lantern, digging finally sitting down, with a trowel, because my six-months pregnant body could no longer manage the balancing act of digging down into the hole and pulling the shovel up carrying dirt. I was a poor lever operator.

Five months ago I nearly killed the thing that will become my baby. Technically again I would not have killed it. And they don't call it killing, not unless they are the sort of people who hold signs outside of clinics with bloody fetuses. They call it *abortion*, or *D&C*, or, most euphemistically, *termination*. I decided not to kill the six-week old collection of cells, though. I decided to keep them and let them grow. This week I read that they now weigh two and a half pounds and have five senses and a full complement of body parts. This seems rather impossible, but apparently it is true.

Nobody ever criticizes you for putting your cat down. Even the most rabid anti-abortion people I know are okay with, as they say, putting an animal out of its suffering. Of course, no one says it's easy, either. Go out and tell people that you had to put your cat or dog to sleep, and you will gain instant sympathy. Post it on a social network and people you barely even know will offer hugs and condolences.

Nobody posts on the internet that she put her embryo down. Many of us, of course, would support her, would offer her strength, would recognize that this, too, may have been a hard decision, or it may have been an easy one, but that the telling of it would not be easy. Because of course many people would not offer such support. They would tell her that she was wrong, that such decisions were not hers to make, that they should be beyond her control.

If you believe that God gave man dominion over all the animals, I suppose it stands to reason that you also feel no particular qualms about having control over their life and death. I never thought I had any particular qualms about it myself. It's true that I don't hunt, but it's also true that I'm not a vegetarian. I kill flies and mosquitoes with impunity, and I feel little regret when I step on ants. Two of my cats died at home, before I had to make any decisions about whether to exercise my control over their lives, or at least over their death. I exercise control over my cats' lives every day: I decide when to feed them; I tell them where they can and cannot go; I clip their claws and give them drugs when the vet prescribes them. But I'd never exercised this particular kind of control before: not the saying yes to the large doses of anesthesia, not the petting and holding the cat for the last time while the vet left me alone in the room with him, not the praying that the baby inside me wouldn't choose that moment, the moment when the syringe hit the cat's leg, as a moment to kick or turn a somersault. That life and death intersect is something I know. But I didn't want them to right then.

A great many people believe that you should not have control over human life, and in some instances, I am one of them—your typical pro-choice, anti-death penalty tax and spend bleeding heart liberal pacifist. No one—least of all the state—should be able to control the ending of another person's life. But the beginning of life—that's where everyone gets hung up.

The issue is often framed as that of who controls a woman's body—the woman, her doctor, the church, the state? The belief, among those I consort with, is that the woman should be in charge. I believe that still, and I will continue to fight for it, but the past six months have led me to understand how little control one actually has.

I used birth control, but it did not work. As a friend of mine says, *birth control* is a misnomer. You're not really in control of the situation. *Contraception* is better—you are trying to prevent something from happening, but it may or may not actually work. To be in the tiny, tiny percentage for whom it does not work is an odd experience, especially at age thirty-five, when you have a professional job and a savings account and are about to become a homeowner. But there you have it: you're not in control. And if you decide, as I did, not to take a certain kind of control at that point, you lose control completely, not only of your body but also of yourself.

I am twenty-eight weeks pregnant as I write this. I weigh thirty-six pounds more than I did six months ago. In those six months, I have been nauseated, fatigued, and dehydrated. My blood sugar has dropped to the point that I've fainted. My whole body has at one or another time hurt, often several parts of it at once. I cannot remember the last time I woke up and felt good, or the last time I leaned over to pick something up or got up from sitting on the floor with anything resembling grace or ease. One goes in that time from pregnancy being a secret that nobody knows—at first, not even you—to a fact on display for everyone, a thing everyone sees and comments on. The baby—and it is a baby now, of a sort—the kind not viable on its own but probably savable by modern medicine—swims around and kicks and punches, and it is supposed to. At the hospital they lecture you: if the baby doesn't move ten times every two hours, something is wrong. That is but one of a long list of things you are instructed to watch out for. If you get a headache or a fever, if you bleed or have stomach pain, if you vomit: all these things are out of your control, and all of them mean you must call the hospital, go in and be put under the control of the machines, the blood pressure cuff, the fetal heart monitor, the ultrasound, the people in scrubs and the people in white coats.

When I fainted, they took me away in an ambulance and put a needle in my arm. Around the other arm they put a blood pressure cuff, and it inflated and deflated every ten minutes. Around my wrist they put a band with my name and hospital number, the same one that was given to me when I was born. Somewhere the very first band with that number is in a baby book my mother made. Eventually, only when they knew that someone was coming to pick me up, they unhooked me and let me go, let me put my own clothes on and walk out the door.

I live now in a house that I bought myself, with money I earned. My old cat is buried here between two trees, where I imagine he watches the birds and feels the squirrels and chipmunks and gazes West toward the sunset, toward the place he came from, where I used to live, and where my other cat is buried. This past week I got two new cats to share my house with me. They have taken control. They jump on tables and counters, investigate behind and underneath the furniture. They run and jump and pounce, sometimes on each other and sometimes on things only they can see. They are, at times, even more active than my baby, who rarely stops moving in my womb. I do not bother to count his kicks—I can tell he is there and doing well.

In twelve more weeks, give or take, I'll be back at the hospital, and my son will be born and get a number of his own. I will not control when that happens, although I hope to control a little bit how it happens: I hope to be there at the hospital with my mother and my doula and some friends. I hope not to be hooked up to machines the whole time, or to be made to lie flat on a bed. I hope to be able to see my son as soon as he is born, perhaps in a fog of pain, but not a fog of painkillers. I hope that my body will perform the way it was made to do, making milk for my baby to drink, but many years ago now I decided to exercise another sort of control: I had a breast reduction to ease the strain on my back, and to have the body that was more like the one I imagined and less like the one I was given. So I don't know yet if the ducts that need to be there for the milk to come have managed to regrow from their severing, or if that particular control I tried to exercise so long ago will mean giving up another thing now.

Let go and let God, say the twelve-step people, whose Serenity Prayer is perhaps the clearest distillation of control that we have. They pray for the strength to change the things one cannot accept and to accept the things they cannot change, and they pray for the wisdom to know the difference.

I walk through life now wondering if there is a difference, or if the surest form of control is simply to accept change. I pray for my son and for myself, for my family and for my friends, but I rarely know any more what to ask for. Peace, I say. Change. Something. Whatever it is we need, if only we could know.

AFTER EASTER

Yesterday I learned that I have "a very healthy four-and-a half-weeks-old-pregnancy." To say that this was a shock is something of an understatement.

I didn't expect to get pregnant. I went to great lengths—a consultation, an office visit, a follow up visit, and $500 plus copays, to get a device that was supposed to keep me from getting pregnant for five years. I checked it religiously every month after my period, as instructed. Sometimes I checked it in between times, just to be sure. I had, in fact, checked it just four days before this pregnancy took hold.

Well. I guess I got a year out of it. I wish the IUD maker would refund me $400, but it doesn't seem to work that way.

After the ultrasound that determined that my IUD was gone and that a sac of cells had implanted itself in the lining of my uterus, I talked with the ob gyn resident who came to see me for a long time. She was wonderful. I want to send her a fan letter. I explained that I couldn't believe this had happened. "I check my strings every month!" I said. "I checked them just four days before this happened!"

"Wow," she said. "In all honesty, I'm not sure I check them every month. Although I think I'm going to start."

We talked about where I could get an abortion, how long I had to decide, what other birth control was available to me if, as she said, "You never want to hear the letters I U D again." She told me to stay on my antidepressants no matter what I decided, and that she took hers all through her pregnancy. She told me about what options I had for care at the hospital if I decided to keep the baby. She laughed at my jokes. I think she would have sat there all day if I needed it.

I have no decision yet, but I just took my first prenatal vitamin, and my first folic acid, as I was told to do in this interim, limbo time, just in case.

The vitamin is oval and fuchsia, like a mini-Hindenburg designed by Kate Spade. The folic acid is a tiny round dull off-white disc. I bought them at Walgreen's over lunch. They are some supposedly "natural" brand, whatever that means. Despite my outward appearances and proclivities, I'm not sure it matters that much. I bought them because they were on sale.

This is the same Walgreen's where, on Tuesday, I bought a pregnancy test, although I don't think I had the same clerk. I was amusing myself with the thought of what kinds of narratives store clerks make up about customers. I did worry today, as I didn't on Tuesday, oddly, that I would run into someone I know. This is my hometown, after all, and it's not all that big. I imagined seeing someone and having them eye me, or better yet ask, and then I imagined what I could say to them. "Not that it's any of your business, but yes, I may in fact be having a baby. Or I may not."

This baby is not by any definition but the very strictest even a baby yet. It is a sac. Even the ultrasound tech at the hospital said they don't call it a baby: the picture they give you is simply titled BABY HOUSE. That's an apt description. I remember the children's book *A House is a House for Me*, and having an assignment to design a house for some sort of animal. I believe mine was for an otter, although I may be imagining myself as more creative than I actually was. It might just have been a home for a cat. It was elaborate, in any case, full of everything I believed the animal might want. One wonders what sort of house the human body makes.

Yesterday my mother said, "Well, you'll have to quit smoking. Or at least cut back," and then we both howled, because of course I don't smoke. I am a failed smoker: I tried to start in college, but it never took. A lot of things suddenly seem quite funny to me.

I failed at breakfast again completely but managed some of lunch, since I was actually hungry, and since the vitamins say to take them with a meal. I ate a bowl of tomato soup with some spinach, and I ate most of the last of the cheese from the reception a few weeks ago. There are still a few squares of cheese and an apple on my plate, but I had to stop. My weight at the hospital yesterday was three pounds less than I thought it was, and less than I've weighed in some years, but my pants still feel tight. Go figure.

Every day brings with it a seemingly obvious choice. Yesterday, talking with my mom, it seemed obvious that I had to have this baby. Today it seems like a terrible thing to do to everyone, myself included. The baby's father said today that he is sorry to bail on me but that he needs a few days to think. I said I could only imagine, and that that was fine, and that he should take all the time he needs. I worry far more about him than I do about me. I have friends and family; he has children and debt. I cannot imagine what a shock this must be, though of course it's nobody's fault. I worry too that people will judge him too harshly, that they will, because they are my friends, invariably take my side, or rather invent a side for me, when I don't feel that I have one. I worry that the situation is so unbelievable that people will want to be angry, and that means they need an object. And they don't know him, so he is the most likely one around. And I can't have that. I know his flaws as well as anyone, but they are not all that make him. And if I do decide to have baby, he will be its father, and I need everyone to accept him, to afford him the respect of that position, as well as the respect any two human beings should show for one another. I told my mother last night that I expected this from my family, that I would, in fact, not tolerate anything else. She said she is on my side, that she has always respected the baby's father, that she will go to bat for me and for him with the rest of the family if necessary.

But I still don't know what I am going to do.

20 MAY: THE FULLNESS OF TIME

I never know what time it is anymore.

This is not listed anywhere as a symptom or side effect of pregnancy, although presumably that's because most people don't actually have a sort of inner clock that allows them almost always to guess the time of day or night within about twenty minutes. I can't say for sure of course if this is related to my condition; I just know that nowadays instead of waking up and thinking, "It's 5:30" or "It's 7" I wake up disoriented and fumbling for my iPod or my phone so I can find out what time it is and whether I need to get up right now or not.

Today I woke up at 6:39. It's Friday, but in practice it's my Saturday, since I work all day tomorrow. A full day on the circulation desk with two coworkers and an hour off for lunch should be interesting. I'm afraid I'll start staring off into space, or crying. Or drooling, which would be even worse.

"The fullness of time" is a phrase that appears multiple times in the Bible, although I'm not sure just how many, nor can I remember all the contexts. But it was also the subject of one of the only sermons I've ever heard that I remember, given by the Rev. Anne Baker, whose funeral I attended just a few weeks ago. She was one of the first women ordained as a priest in the Episcopal Church, back in 1977, and she was the associate rector at my church when I was a kid. I acolyted for her many times.

This particular sermon must have been when I was eleven or twelve, and it started with a story she had read in the news recently about a woman giving birth after a gestation of only four or five month—I can't remember the details, but it was much, much shorter than a normal pregnancy would be. Anne talked about how strange and frightening that must have been, and she talked about Biblical examples of the fullness of time, and she talked about patience. What I took from it—what I remember, nearly 25 years later, is that her sermon was about how certain things take time, and you have to grant that time. Sometimes the time is known—nine months for a pregnancy, four years for high school, 24 hours for a stomach flu—and sometimes it is not. But that time, and that waiting, is important: it is part of the process.

People in the Bible are constantly being asked to wait, and they are also constantly asked the impossible. And sometimes they are asked the impossible only to be asked something very different just moments later. Abraham and Isaac are the prime example here: God asks Abraham to sacrifice Isaac. Then he asks him not to. Abraham has a choice, presumably, the first time. He could choose disobedience, but he doesn't, which infuriates many people, although I suspect mostly people are pissed off at God, not at Abraham. But the thing about the story is that it asks you to live with these two very different ideas and with a very, very hard idea. You can see where I'm going with this: that's just how I feel now. And it's terrifying.

So I back away from Abraham and Isaac a little bit and I think about the fullness of time. I think about the angels who come to people and say, "Fear not," which, as a character in one of Madeleine L'Engle's books points out, gives you some idea of what angels must actually have looked like. Terrifying. Not the woman with wings on the stained glass window at my church, her hands and face stiff with holiness.

I did not get an angel coming to me. I got a line on a plastic stick on in the restroom at work, in between training someone on the new cash register software and going to a coordinators' meeting. The package says that your results will appear within two minutes after you pee on the stick, but mine showed up almost instantly, that blue line forming, at first faintly but unmistakably. It was, I suppose, equally frightful. I wrote a few years ago that if Jesus were here today, perhaps he would be saying that the Kingdom of Heaven is like unto a plastic bottle, and so perhaps today's angels also come in the form of plastic.

My stomach is growling a little, but I can't think of anything I could stand to eat, although coffee still tastes good, thank God. The baby's father asked if I would like to come over for a bit today—he has his 2.5 year old son, and we had promised him on Wednesday that we would show him my green Honda today. I have been driving a green Volvo that belongs to the people I am house-sitting for, but my real car is finally fixed. Mr. 2.5 loves cars and is learning all their parts, and he can recognize all kinds of cars by their shapes from a distance. So: shower, get dressed, go over for a bit. At ten I have a massage appointment with C, and then I need to buy a birthday present for her about to be Ms. 12, and then I have a therapy appointment and a coffee date. The time today is mostly full, and that is good. The readiness is all.

21 MAY: NOT IDEAS ABOUT THE THING BUT THE THING ITSELF

The more you talk about the baby as a baby, the more, of course, it seems like it might be a baby. But in order to talk about it you have to call it something, and you have to call everyone else involved something, too. The baby's father called it Person X the other day in a message, which I rather like, except of course that that, too, involves a certain personhood. My whole relationship to the baby's father is so unclear at the moment that it seems most accurate to describe him as the father, a relationship defined by his relation to Person X, not his relationship to me.

But for all that I use terms that imply an existence, I truly have no idea what the baby—Person X—it—is. I saw the ultrasound: at the moment, it is a sac attached to the side of my uterus. Biologically speaking, it's something more than that—a zygote or some other term I once learned in biology or health class but have long since forgotten, thinking it wasn't ever going to apply to me.

This isn't intended as a foray into the question of when life begins, or What is Life?, or any of those other things that religious and political figures like to debate. All that seems completely irrelevant to me and my situation. The political realities of it aren't, of course—I keep thinking about what I'd be going through if this had happened in Wyoming. No Emma Goldman Clinic or Planned Parenthood just across town, but a two and a half hour drive to another state, and having to arrange time off from work, and someone to drive me, and yet at the same time trying to keep it all a secret—it would be hell, and I suddenly realize just how hard this is for many women—practically hard, not just philosophically hard. But the dialogue of abortion seems about as far from what I'm going through as a discussion of the colonization of Mars, or whether there should be playoff for one of those college ball tournaments, which is, to judge by the reporting on NPR, actually an issue of major national importance. I barely even listen to the news anymore. I gather that Obama is talking to Israel and that the head of the IMF is in what sounds like well-deserved deep shit, but that's about it.

Last night my mother told me that when she finally realized it would be easier to raise me without my father, she was able to sleep properly for the first time in weeks. I suppose the lesson there is that sometimes these decisions take weeks, but of course it is a hard thing to hear. I grew up mostly without my father, although that was not my mother's fault, or, really, his. I've never been to a suicide survivor's group because it seems they all function around a particular set of emotions you are supposed to have: that, for instance, you need to heal your anger at the person who killed himself. I can't relate. I'm not been angry at my father, and I've never understood the tendency of people to be angry at suicides or those who attempt it. Would you be angry at someone for having a heart attack? A stroke? I suppose you might be angry if a diabetic died or suffered serious complications because she was irresponsible about managing her diabetes, but surely that would not be your only, or even strongest, reaction. Or maybe not. Maybe I am an anomaly.

In fifteen minutes I have to go work the last two hours of my shift for the day. I have, rather miraculously, avoided having to run to the bathroom twice an hour all day, but it's strange to be working in close proximity to other people and not have them know, to know that my body is not the body it was just a month ago, that I must make a decision about it, and that that, too, might end up being a secret. Or not a secret to anyone at all.

21 MAY: SATURDAY NIGHT'S

I have rarely in my life wanted a glass of wine as badly as I want one now. Oh hell. I don't just want a glass: I'd happily put away the better part of a bottle. And of course I can't. This kid, if a kid indeed it turns out to be, got plenty of secondhand vino in its first month when I was off visiting Missouri and having dinners with poets and mystics and so on. I'm not going to worry about that, but at this point it's like the prenatal vitamins and the folic acid: it'd be good for the kid if a kid it is, and it really is not bad for me. Just tiresome.

I ate an enormous amount of dinner in order to make up for the lack of accompaniment. It was a chicken with spinach and Indian spices dish over rice, and it was delicious. But one serving would have been plenty.

I rarely do anything on a Saturday night but sit at home and make dinner and listen to Saturday night radio programs—"A Prairie Home Companion" and the guy who plays old rock and roll for three hours after that. Saturdays in the past month have been the exception. And a dinner party right now would be out of the question. I'm exhausted, among other things, and I can't quite imagine the possibility of company. I love my friends and my family, but right now I can't handle their speculation on top of my own.

So I'm trying to write all this down and then forget about it and read my book and go to bed. That may or may not work—my latest obsession, of course, is running numbers in my head. I was doing this before as I thought about buying a house. Now, of course, it's doubled, almost literally: mortgage + daycare + student loan + absolutes = not much left to buy food, much less clothing or, God forbid, music or dinner out. I can do that; I've done it before. And I will have help. But it's a lot, and the math is suddenly all very different.

I keep thinking of the line from the Greg Brown song that I started thinking about in early April—"passion seemed to promise more than friendship can endure," and I keep hoping it's one of those lines that applies only in literature and not in my own life.

22 MAY: NOISE AND SILENCE

I'm supposed to be writing my theatre column, but since it's not technically due until tomorrow sometime, and since it is for a publication that has yet to send me my first paycheck, and since I have compiled a list of all the things I need to write about, and since, well, I AM GOING THROUGH A MAJOR LIFE CRISIS, I am putting that aside for now.

Today's been one of the days where, despite the talk of my friends, I mostly think OMG WTF I CAN'T POSSIBLY HAVE A BABY. Partly, of course, this is that things with the baby's father are so uncertain at the moment and seem to becoming more so daily, although he did dash over here to mow my lawn, and he did, in addition to getting my car from the shop and changing its oil last week also wash it inside and out, which seems kind of above and beyond. All I ever do at his house is the dishes. But then he likes cars and I mostly think of them as a major pain except when they are running and I need them, in which case, of course, they are wonderful.

One of my two oldest friends was here again last night, and I made pancakes for her for breakfast again (with the obligatory barefoot and pregnant over a hot stove joke) this morning. She said, "You know, if you're up for it, if you decide to have the baby, you could go to Birthright and make them give you a bunch of free stuff." Birthright is one of those horrible places where they lure you in with free pregnancy tests and then tell you about the horrors of abortion but, apparently, also give you cribs and diapers and things. I can't even stand the thought of those people, and while I'm all for screwing over the system, there's a limit to what I can endure.

This afternoon was the birthday of my other oldest friend's oldest daughter, who just turned twelve. We started in the park a couple blocks from where I'm living, but then the tornado sirens started going off, so we all came here. Three hours of nine kids between the ages of four and twelve plus their assorted parental units and my friend's crazy mother and rapid air pressure shifts and sirens was almost more than I could bear, and I kept thinking, *Dear God, I cannot do this. Any of it.* And I love my friend's kids with all my heart, but, as you can see in the picture of me from the party she just posted on Facebook, I was almost dead from anxiety and despair and trying to calm parents during a storm and keep their children safe and entertained and dry. I failed at that last one completely, but luckily there are a lot of towels in this house.

After they all left, at long last, I replied, poorly, to the baby's father's latest email, and then I made myself eat some dinner and take my vitamins, and then I wept and shook. When your choices boil down to "have a glass of wine or kill myself," the glass of wine, even if you're pregnant, seems like it might be the better solution. Another friend told me once that she was looking for a tree to drive into once but then decided she couldn't do it because she was in my car. Our other friend said, when she told him, "I really think that would be the least of Laura's concerns," and that's very true, but when you're mentally ill, I think you have to take moments of grace in whatever form they come, even if they aren't the healthiest.

Then I decided I should call A. She's the only real mutual friend that the baby's father and I have and is thus, unlike most of my friends, I feel, less likely to dismiss him out of hand. As I've said, I simply cannot tolerate that. This is no one's fault, and I was raised by a mother and grandmother who often demonized men. They have good reason—their stories aren't identical, but they both married alcoholics who ultimately killed themselves. That's enough to put anyone off. But I can't live my life that way. I won't. The baby's father isn't perfect, and I won't absolve him of all responsibility, but I won't have him made into the bad guy, without any consideration given to his feelings in the whole matter. Among other things, he has said unequivocally that if I decide to keep this pregnancy, he will help out and has, in fact, already volunteered for childcare three days a week. That can't be easy for him, and yet he's said it.

So I talked to A for nearly two hours. She, too, is gung-ho about my having a baby. Actually, it seems like everyone feels that way except for the baby's father and me, and we both vacillate, frequently. I'm not sure what that says. But we talked about the baby's father and about the pregnancy and about God and therapy and a dozen other things, and in the end I was able to get off the phone and eat some fruit and yogurt and make the list of all the theatre stuff I need to write about, which it looks like I'll somehow do at work tomorrow. It's a good thing, as I've said, that they think I've gotten so much done at work, because other than working my desk shifts and training people on cash register software, I'm doing diddly-squat these days.

Right now it's nine pm, and I'm exhausted even after twelve hours of sleep last night. I feel as though I could spend all my time these days sleeping, feeling pukey, eating, or crying. I'm striving to make sleeping the biggest part of that. It's avoidant, I know, but it's also healing. Or so I can only hope. Sleep, and prayer.

24 MAY: GOODNIGHT NOBODY

No baby.

It simply can't be. I'll call for an appointment as soon as the clinic opens later today.

Partly it was the growing feeling of dread, partly it was a talk with the baby's father yesterday evening, partly it is the overall sense of impossibility, and the belief that it would destory the baby's father's life and be unfair to the rest of his children.

So. Decision made.

I will go back to my what I was before. I will be okay.

25 MAY: THE WORLD IS TOO MUCH WITH US

I have an appointment for next Wednesday. And, apparently, I still have uncertainty, or at least other people do. And I am sick with a bad cold, on top of everything else, which seems like not the prime time to be making a serious decision, or reconsidering a serious decision, or whatever it is that I am currently trying to do.

Yesterday I told everybody, or everybody who knows. Many of the people who had heretofore not expressed opinions suddenly had them, although not all. I suppose there's a psychological effect at work there—if you think I should have the baby and I decide to have the baby, you will say so; if you think I should not and I do not, you will say so. That makes sense.

The baby's father seems worried that termination would unhinge me. I told him I already feel unhinged, and I'm not sure what would make it better or worse.

The baby's father's sister sent me a wonderful email yesterday after I told her of my decision, saying that it must be tremendously hard, but that it was the right one. A called today to reiterate her feeling that this baby is meant to be, and that I cannot take the baby's father into account, that I have to make the decision for myself.

I hate that. It's easier to take other people into account. It relieves me of so much, but I know it's the lazy way out.

I always thought my father dying was the worst thing that would ever happen to me, and I felt lucky, because it had already happened. I hadn't counted on anything like this kind of decision and its lifelong consequences. I hadn't counted on the fact that once pregnant, all my feelings would change. I hadn't ever counted on love until last month, and even then I was trying not to, but I failed, and then of course that failed, too.

I do not know what to do.

26 MAY: COUNSEL

Last night I talked on the phone with the baby's father twice. We never talk on the phone, but I have told him I can't have in depth discussions via email or Facebook or text message, particularly not when I'm at work. He is on a break between spring semester and summer session, so he has plenty of preparation to do but no real time that he has to show up and do it, and while I don't mean to diminish the seriousness and difficulty of his work, it is not, at least at the moment, really comparable to having to be in charge of people and programs and work with the public, which is what I do for forty hours a week, at least when I am not sick. I have to go in for at least a few hours today, and then I have an appointment with my psychiatrist, and then I may very well come back home and sleep.

Anyway, we had these difficult phone conversations, largely because he had left me a message about a discussion with his lawyer and his worry that terminating the pregnancy would unhinge me. So I called and we talked about that, among other things.

After that first conversation I sent a message to A that was so apparently desperate and discombobulated that she called on her way to a party and told me I needed to stop talking to him altogether. Then I talked to other friends, on the phone and IM, and somehow in the midst of that got my theatre column written, which was a great weight off my mind. And then I called the baby's father back to ask him two questions and to tell him that I loved him but couldn't really talk to him anymore, that while this had been a decision I had wanted to make together, it was clear I needed to make it on my own, and that his waffling about everything wasn't helping that.

But that didn't seem like the right thing either, and then I hit on an idea. I would be willing to talk to him, I said, but only if we did so in the presence of a couples counselor or some other third, neutral party. I am feeling too vulnerable right now, and while my conversations with the baby's father have been civil—no arguments, no accusations—I need the protection of a witness, and I think perhaps the baby's father needs that, too. I don't know. Couples counseling always seems like one of those things people throw money at because they're unwilling to deal with the reality that their relationship is over. Our relationship is already over. Is there such a thing as ex-couples therapy? It seems stupid, I guess, but it also seems worth a try.

I am rereading *Hard Laughter*, which I checked out Tuesday from the library. I think it may be the same copy I first read nearly eleven years ago, after the first debacle with the baby's father. And yes, that's how long this has been going on. Nearly a third of my life. You'd think I might have learned. Or that we both might have.

I'm happy to be writing again, though. Not this, so much, which is more typing than writing, but there are bits of it, and there is the essay I am working on about altered landscapes. I never thought my own body would be one of them.

Oh, but the other thing—before I hung up last night, I remembered a story my mother just told me that I wanted to tell the baby's father, about how my father had taught a professor we both know many years ago, and how after he came out here, he contacted my father, who didn't really remember him, but my parents invited him and his then wife out for dinner anyway, though it was sort of awkward. "No wonder he doesn't really like me," I said. "I always thought it was just because I wasn't blonde, but this explains so much." The baby's father laughed, as I knew he would, and as only he could, because he knows the person in question, and knows about my father, and knows my other story about this professor, who, when he saw me at a party at the end of my first year in graduate school, asked me if my father still taught at the college up north. "No," I said, "my father died in 1981." You lived a block away from us, I wanted to say. How the hell did you miss this? He killed himself, for God's sake, and it was in the paper, and this is a small town. Good God.

And that's the thing. There are plenty of people I can tell that story to, but few who understand all its nuances, who get the absurdities of it, in the way that the baby's father does.

But I am trying to guard myself. I know that isn't everything. He sent me three texts last night and this morning, and I have not responded. Today I start looking for a couples' counselor.

27 MAY: THE ELEPHANT ALSO STARTED THIS WAY

I feel so very and incredibly alone.

I know that isn't really true. My mother is arriving shortly, and we are going to my grandmother's for the weekend, and my great aunt and favorite older cousin are coming as well, and I have friends who've checked in via email and IM and phone today, and there are people praying for me.

But I feel alone, alone in this big house with my terrible cold and my fever and my morning sickness and the cat who won't stop peeing places and the dishes and the trash and the mail that keeps arriving and the horrible carpet and the uncomfortable furniture.

Of course, I'm sick, and that brings out my worst I am all alone in the world and nobody really cares for me feelings even at the best of times. I did the dishes at the baby's father's house the last time I saw him, Monday night I guess, because he'd made dinner, and I said that I firmly believed that the person who cooks should not also have to do dishes.

"I usually do both," he said.

"So do I," I said, "because I live by myself and almost always have." But I think that when there is more than one person, you should split that up. But in my life there mostly has just been me. If I keep this pregnancy, there will be another person, but not one who can help out, not for many years. I think about how I supposedly "helped" by setting the table and microwaving the vegetable starting when I was about six, but I know now how pitiful an amount that really is. I know how hard it would be to be by myself but with a kid.

I also know people do it, including the baby's father, who takes care of his other children part-time, solo, and always has. And I know how I felt on Tuesday, when I thought I'd made a decision, and suddenly everywhere I went there were pregnant women, and each one of those round perfect forms was like a stab in the gut with a sharp knife.

I told myself I wouldn't think about this while I was sick, and while I am waiting for our couples counseling appointment on Tuesday afternoon, and while I am with my family this weekend, but obviously I am failing. The elephant in the room is very, very tiny now, but in my mind, it's massive; it's like the whole world.

29 MAY: FAMILY, AND FAT ON CARBS

"Look at it this way," I said to my grandmother, as I was flipping over the two-year-old article on toxic debts she'd just given me from *The Week,* out of curiosity, to see what was on the back side, "at least if I have the baby, it won't have John Edwards being the father and claiming he's not."

She and my mother and I howled.

If there's an agnostic's version of immaculate conception, my grandmother's response to the news (and she, like everyone, immediately knew what it was going to be as soon as I said, "I have to tell you something." Is there anything else those words ever mean when coming from a single 35-year-old woman? Apparently not) was to rejoice in the miracle of the possibility of another child in the family, although she, like everyone, was quick to qualify and reiterate that it was My Decision and that she Supports Me No Matter What I Do.

She's of course not thrilled with the idea of the baby's father as the father, though she promised that if she could be polite to my grandfather, she could be polite to him. Well. There are worse endorsements, I suppose. I mean, she could have said, "If I can be polite to George Bush, I can be polite to him." At least she respected my grandfather's intellect. Then again, she's never been called upon to be polite to George Bush.

It's a great weight off my mind to have told her, and though I believed she would be supportive, and that she would not care, it is a great relief nonetheless to hear her say that she does not care that I am not married, or that the child, if there is one, would have a single parent, and so on.

In a way her experience is close to my own: she was in love with my grandfather still, and perhaps always, and she had to steel herself against him. Imagine the man you loved asking you repeatedly to marry him again, and having to say no, not unless you quit drinking? I'm not sure I could do it.

We talked, and then because I was still hungry, even though it was nearly nine o'clock at night, she made me scrambled eggs, and I ate them. Then we all read for awhile, and then Mom and I went back to the hotel, where, because I was still hungry, my mother went to get me potato chips and pretzels from the vending machine. I felt bad even asking her, but I'd just gotten out of the shower, and since of course what I really want is a giant bowl of pasta (fettucine alfredo would be ideal, but really any sort of pasta with some cheese would do me nicely), which would be extremely hard to obtain at ten-thirty on a Sunday night, potato chips from the vending machine seemed like an okay thing to ask for. And it's simple, and it's something she can do. This is one of those situations where people seem desperately to want to do things for me, and mostly they can't, because most of what I want is beyond the golden apples of the sun and the silver apples of the moon. The only other things I want are potato chips, and macaroni and cheese, and chicken tetrazini, and scrambled eggs, and pasta, and more pasta, and more cheese. Oh, and vegetables and fruit juice. There should really be a macaroni and cheese delivery service. I would pay good money, and I generally strive to be a frugal sort.

30 MAY: LONG LAST HAPPY

I am, at long last, happy to say that I am going to have a baby.

I know I said exactly the opposite thing last week.

I will write more about all of it later—so this isn't really a last entry, but it's a last entry in this part, this uncertainty, doubt, fear, trepidation, waiting.

No more waiting—or rather, waiting now for something very different to arrive.

11 JUNE: THE ORDEAL AND THE CREATION

Tomorrow is Pentecost, my favorite major holiday of the church year, and so last Sunday was the Ascension, when Jesus, having come back from the dead to do a few last things here on earth, finally ascends into Heaven to sit at the right hand of the father. This was the beginning of the epistle for last Sunday, from the first letter of Peter:

> Beloved, do not be surprised at the fiery ordeal that is taking place among you to test you, as though something strange were happening to you. But rejoice insofar as you are sharing Christ's sufferings, so that you may also be glad and shout for joy when his glory is revealed.

The Bible, I suppose, is sort of like astrology in that it's possible to see its applications to your own life as a matter of simple confirmation bias. The difference, for me, is that, much to the regret of my grandmother, I believe in the Bible (which is only a step away from believing in astrology, in her worldview), and so last Sunday that's what jumped out at me. Something strange is happening to me. Or not strange—it is, in fact, a thoroughly normal thing to happen to a young woman—but it feels strange, nonetheless, and, particularly at the times when I think I'm going to puke, or when I am so tired I can barely sit upright, or when I think that if I don't get something to eat in the next thirty seconds I may collapse, it does feel very much like an ordeal.

My midwife said to me, when I told her how strange and astounding it was to feel so different even this early, that it is indeed amazing, and that if you think about it, it's no wonder that there were so many centuries of legal practice designed to keep from giving women power, because we already had this tremendous power that nobody else did, the power to create new life. That my midwife can say things like this and not make me gag is a function either of her general awesomeness or the fact that she works at the hospital and wears a white coat and thus has the trappings of what I have always associated with a kind of authority and a decided lack of woo-woo.

My father believed that women were intellectually inferior to men, although he also thought they were holy and mystic due to their ability to bear children. As a result, I've always had a distinct aversion to the idea that there's anything remotely special about the ability to bear children. In my undergraduate thesis, I even quoted from a bit of Plato that talked about how one's intellectual works were actually far better than any human children one could produce, which I liked because at that point in my life, I planned to produce intellectual and creative works and not children. Most anyone, it seemed to me, could have a kid, but how many people could write something truly beautiful?

The baby's father said to me awhile ago that it seemed to him that I used to approach the world as a series of concrete blocks that I had to destroy, but that now I approach it more as a series of people to whom I am and must be connected. I've been thinking about that a lot, because there are still a lot of concrete blocks that I'd like to destroy. I ran away from a great many of them—first I got involved in radical politics, which meant I was able to live in a community that shared my ideals, that relied on alternative media, that understood, intrinsically, all the things that I thought were wrong with the way the world worked. Then, when I got too caught up in that, so that it seemed to be taking over my life, I ran away to Wyoming, to a place where everyone was kind of an outsider, and where people seemed content to let me be my own strange self without trying to fight it or expecting me to be anything different. Oh, they thought I was peculiar, to be sure, but they were tolerant of peculiarity, and that was a great relief.

Being pregnant means I am creating something out of my control, beyond my will, something that might grow up to hate the things I love and love the things I hate. And it forces me to some extent back into that very culture I tried so hard to fight against. Oh sure, there are parents who insist on gender-neutral clothing and toys for their children, and who enforce certain dietary and restrictions and adhere to certain politically charged modes of child-rearing. I can decide to raise my child as I was raised, without soft drinks in the house, with minimal television watching, with making things instead of buying them. But the child will be its own person, not a thing under my control as the words I type in this screen are. And I can hardly think of anything more big and terrifying and strange than that. I look forward to seeing what happens.

PENTECOST

Father Bob, my confirmation teacher (and also for many years The Voice of the Hawkeyes on one local radio station) told us that the Gospel of John was (and I believe this is an exact quotation) "just weird," and that it therefore did not have its own year in the Lectionary the way that Matthew, Mark, and Luke do but was instead scattered about and saved for special occasions. I perceived at the time that this must mean John was the underdog, and so it became my favorite Gospel. I later realized that my perception of John as the underdog was about as accurate as my perception of Beatrice and Benedick as minor characters in *Much Ado About Nothing*, which is the first Shakespeare I ever saw on stage, around that same time. But it's still my favorite Gospel.

It is, though, weird. All the others start out in a rather normal (for the Bible) narrative fashion, naming people and their relatives and their descendants, or telling you about John the Baptist, or beginning, essentially, "Once upon a time." But John starts with this: *In the beginning was the Word.*

Then he tells you that the Word is with God and that the Word is God. It's like the Beatles got mixed up with the literary theory people, and it's all the more confusing if you know Greek and realize the number of possible translations for each prepositional phrase, even in *koine* Greek, what some professor of my mother's called "a late, demotic form." Or perhaps that was Medieval Latin he was referring to. Anyway. It's sort of crazy.

And it's crazier still because it's such a human idea—that you can't have a thing without a word for the thing, and

26

that therefore the first thing you have to have in the beginning is a word—the Word.

We don't actually read that Gospel on Pentecost. Today we read about Jesus breathing the Holy Spirit onto the disciples, and in the earlier lessons about Moses receiving the Holy Spirit and the great one from Acts about everyone speaking in their own tongues, and Peter quoting to everyone the words of Joel about the last days: "and your young men shall see visions, and your old men shall dream dreams." Some years, although not this one, we also read my very favorite passage in the Bible, the bit from 1st Corinthians about the variety of gifts.

In the passage from Acts, the tongues are remarkable not because of the Babel/babble they create, but because each person there can hear clearly their own language. In my church, we always do something in different languages simultaneously—sometimes one of the lessons; this year the Lord's Prayer—and so it is a cacophony, a whole series of voices from which it is impossible to pick one strand. A stranger walking into the church would think indeed that we were all simply speaking in tongues, and might be mightily confused, since Episcopalians don't tend to go in for that sort of thing.

We do like our words, though. Someone a few years back published a piece about the Anglican Communion in *The New Yorker*, the gist of which was that we were a denomination that cared very little about what you actually thought so long as you just used *The Book of Common Prayer*. It's a slightly cruel characterization, but it's not an inaccurate one. I love church not wholly but largely because I love the liturgy, and I love the liturgy because I love the language. *Almighty God to you all hearts are open, all desires known, and from you no secrets are hid. May the peace of the Lord be among you now and remain with you always.* You hear these words at the opening and at the closing of the service each Sunday, and it's deeply comforting and very beautiful. You are welcomed, wholly, all of you known, and then you are sent out into the world forgiven, loved, and free, sent out to do the work you have been given to do, with something like the Force to guide you and be with you always.

But I'd never thought much about what it meant to be a people of the Word until Pentecost today, which included, as it often does, several baptisms. Every week in the Nicene Creed, and today in the renewal of baptismal vows, we avow that the Lord Jesus Christ was conceived by the power of the Holy Spirit and became incarnate through the Virgin Mary. You'd think that in thirty-five years of off-and-on church attendance, I might before have paid attention to how deeply weird that is, but it never struck me. Conceived by the power of the Holy Spirit? That thing that causes tongues of flame to dance around on people's foreheads, and makes them speak in different languages? That Holy Spirit? Pardon my language, but what the fuck? All possible puns intended.

Of course the Baby Jesus, whose body and blood we eat and drink every week, isn't exactly a normal person and thus wasn't conceived in the normal way, but we tell ourselves stories in order to live, and if, like me, you are pregnant and rather surprised and alarmed by it all, it's perhaps natural to want to relate your condition to that of the most famous surprising and alarming pregnancy of all time.

In the beginning, I met this baby's father, and we exchanged words. Many, many words, over the years, which we are still exchanging. The couples counselor, on hearing that I was writing about my experiences, said to the baby's father., "Oh, and do you journal, too?" It's to our great credit that we both didn't storm out then, screaming at the top of our lungs, "JOURNAL IS NOT A VERB!" We barely even exchanged an eyeroll. We were very, very good, and the baby's father explained that he wrote poems and essays, and that this would doubtless be a very well documented child. I picture the therapist, bless hear heart, imagining rhymed couplets printed on paper with teddy bears. But perhaps I am just being mean.

෴෴෴

In Greg Brown's "Spring Wind," the old couple burn their love letters so their children won't be shocked. What I will have to burn, baby, is something very different. I offer up any doubts that I would ever have you to the Holy Spirit, in the hopes that the Spirit will take them with grace, and will let you know over time that you were loved from the moment of your creation, from the word unto the word made flesh.

13 JUNE: TERMINOLOGY

I was about to go to bed and then realized that I hadn't written anything today, or that all I'd written was a medium length furious unsent email, which has its place, but isn't really what I want to be writing. And in the midst of all the theology here, I have not covered much in the way of practical details, so here goes.

What my friend calls the "morning (read all day)" sickness seems mostly to be under control, so long as I get a lot of sleep and eat every two hours or so while I'm awake. I never thought eating would be a chore, but when you have to do it as frequently as I do, it starts to seem that way. I'm mostly too tired to cook, and so it's just a constant scramble for calories. I am truly surprised that my bridesmaid's dress still fits.

Last week I had my first appointment with the nurse-midwife, hereafter called simply the midwife for the sake of simplicity. My grandmother was greatly intrigued at the whole notion: I was explaining that there are four midwives, and you have a primary one, but you see them all, because whichever one is on duty when you go into labor is the one who catches the baby. But unless your pregnancy gets complicated, or there's some kind of major emergency, you only see the midwives, not the usual endless parade of doctors and residents and medical students you get at the hospital. I am all in favor of teaching hospitals, but given that I've been acting as a teaching hospital subject since I was in preschool, I kind of figure I can take some time off from that business now.

The first appointment is mostly just talking, although I also peed in a cup and got blood drawn, and now, thanks to the wonders of their new fangled electronic medical records system, I can look at my results online. They are totally inscrutable to me, since they don't bother to translate them into anything I would actually understand, such as "you are totally fine!" or "you have an infection, but we will cure it!" I had to ask my mom, because I was kind of freaked out by it all. According to her I am borderline anemic, but that's what they tell me half the time when I go to give blood, too, so that's hardly surprising. I assume if there's something I actually need to worry about, someone will tell me. In the meantime, though, I have to wonder if this fancy new system is really helping them out at all. Doesn't it probably just result in frantic phone calls from patients wondering what the hell all those numbers in their chart mean?

The worst part of it, though, from my perspective, is that when I click on the overview, I get a list of current Health Issues, which reads like this:

> PRENATAL CARE
> PERSONAL HISTORY OF ALLERGY TO
> PENICILLIN
> SECOND OR MORE PREGNANCY IN A
> WOMAN 35 YEARS OR OLDER
> POSTOPERATIVE STATE
> UNPLANNED PREGNANCY/SINGLE PARENT

I have no notion of how I get the "second or more pregnancy," since I've never been pregnant, and it's a little unclear to me how prenatal care qualifies as a health issue, but of course it's that last one that gets to me. *Unplanned pregnancy/single parent.* My mother says this is why they all hate the stupid online health record, because it's reductive, and it makes patients feel like shit. That's my word, not hers, but it is how I feel.

"It makes you feel like a dumb teenager," she said. "No," I said, "it makes me feel like a dumb 35-year-old, which is worse. At least people expect teenagers to be dumb."

I know that the people of the world tend to consider visibly pregnant women to be their property—theirs to advise, critique, touch, whatever. I'm a ways off from that point, so now I just feel like the property of my friends and family, whose opinions range from overjoyed to befuddled. And now I'm the property of the health care system, too, which has its own set of views of me. I know that the doctor I saw at my first visit and the midwife I saw last week don't see me as just Unplanned pregnancy/single parent. I didn't feel in any way when I was talking to them that that's what they thought of me. But of course they have to cooperate with a records system full of controlled vocabulary—something my librarian friends will recognize as useful but frequently evil. We need to collocate things on a subject. You want all the books on, say, knitting to come up together, and so you assign them to some chosen term, regardless of whether or not that word appears in the title. It's the opposite of the way most people are used to searching now, when we plunk words into boxes on the internet and hope to come up with something relevant. But even Google, for all its cleverness, is still matching letters in a row, not determining aboutness. The knitting example is benign, but many terms are less so. Do you choose Burma or Myanmar for the name of the country? How do you decide to refer to groups of people—gays? homosexuals? Are lesbians their own category, and what about the rest of the LGBTQ spectrum? You need to choose some term to make cataloging and searching possible. But the term isn't chosen by the real experts—by the people it describes, or by the people looking for that information. It's chosen in a far off, almost clinical place, a cubicle in some database vendor's headquarters, or some catacomb at the Library of Congress.

And the results are sometimes not at all good, but we have to work with them.

I've spent much of my life fighting the terms I've been defined by. Now I will have even more to resist.

14 JUNE: BIGFOOT

Yoga and then dinner at my mom's and then taking a shower because I realized I hadn't recently means it is suddenly very late. I was on the verge of leaving Mom's an hour before I did, but then our friend L, who is staying with her, got back from her dinner, and so we all chatted, which was good. It may be better for me not to spend entire evenings by myself at home, even though those used to be my favorite sorts of evenings of all.

For dinner we had steak and potatoes and mushrooms and broccoli and sliced tomatoes. No one can say that this kid and I aren't eating well, that's for sure. I just wish I had the energy to do more cooking. I can only hope the baby ends up liking to take naps on the weekends so I can get food made for the week. I realize this will be kind of a nightmare, but obviously people do it, so it must be doable.

Today I had terrible back pain, and, at K's urging, I called the OB nurse. "Hi," I said to the receptionist who answered the phone, "I'm a freaked out pregnant lady."

"Well, we all need a hobby," she said.

I was told to do Tylenol and ice and for sure see my massage therapist if I wanted, but to call them back immediately if I had spotting or cramping.

The first person I talked to—the "we all need a hobby" person—said perhaps it was just a very well-aimed kick. I said I was fairly sure it wasn't actually big enough to kick yet, but L suggested later that perhaps in addition to its developing internal organs and whatnot, it also has a very big foot. I'm tremendously amused by the picture of this giant head, no body to speak of, giant foot. It's almost enough to want to go in for the ultrasound, but thankfully I've had no further problems, so that shouldn't be necessary.

I have real estate stuff to read and prenatal testing stuff to read and *Mad Men* to watch and of course books I actually want to read, not to mention dishes to put in the dishwasher and a house to clean, but it's later than I should be up already, and so I'm just going to go to bed.

15 JUNE: THE DOING

I am trapped, depending on which of my friends you talk to, in a circle of hell, a telenovela, a Dickens novel, or a soap opera. Actually, I'm fairly sure all of those qualify as circles of hell, and Dickens is the lowest. My loathing for Dickens is well-known, if inexplicable. My mother hates Hemingway for similar non-reasons; the baby's father hates Milton, although he said a couple of months ago that he was coming around on Milton, or at least some of Milton. It may be just Paradise Lost that he hates. I love Paradise Lost. My mother loves Dickens. There are people who love Hemingway, although I don't think I'm close to any of them.

But I digress.

It seems that the baby's father's ex, the mother of his Mr. 2.5, and her new partner want to buy the same house I want to buy.

He's mentioned this to me but not to them. He and my mom both think I should just go ahead and go for it. I foresee a giant mess. Although, really, at this point, what does it matter? I look forward to being a scandal; I might as well be a hissing, too.

I just finished rereading Anne Lamott's *All New People*, which may actually be my favorite of her novels, although it's hard to say. It seemed applicable in this instance since one of the few things that happens in the books is that the main character's uncle sleeps a few times with a friend while (as it turns out) temporarily separated from his wife, and the friend gets pregnant, and this is the early 1960s, and the friend is Catholic and won't have an abortion, and the uncle ends up going back to his wife, and—well, you get the picture. But because it is an Anne Lamott book and not a Thomas Hardy book, everybody turns out broken but more or less okay. (It will be a long, long time before I reread *Tess of the d'Urbervilles*.)

I am a great rereader of books. It may be my number one talent. And one of the more cheerful thoughts I have these days is of all the books I will get to reread to my kid someday—all the books my mother read to me when I was five and six and seven and eight. All the Oz books, and *The Five Little Peppers and How They Grew*, and *The Wheel on the School*, and *The Good Master*. I will not make the kid guess all the riddles in *The Hobbit*, so that it takes a week just to get through that chapter, but we'll read it, for sure.

I realize I'm getting ahead of myself, and that there will be many years of intolerable picture books over and over again before we get to any of this, and that the kid may well hate all these obscure old books that I loved, but I have to think of something.

My mother read all those books to me after my father died, and every Monday night we ate dinner at a card table in the living room so we could watch *M*A*S*H*. I did not understand very much about the show at the time. I didn't understand that it was set during Korea but it was really about Vietnam. I didn't know what Vietnam was, and wouldn't for many years, though I'd later become obsessed with it. I didn't know what homosexuality was, or what a Section 8 was, or that my father was discharged from the army in WWII under some similar section, not because he was gay but because they thought he was crazy. I just knew that the man who dressed in women's clothes was funny, and that Radar was from Iowa, just like me, and that Hawkeye was tall and funny like my dad, and a doctor like my mom was becoming, and that my mother was a little bit in love with him.

We ate a lot of soufflés at that card table. I suppose they were quick and cheap, but they're not something I remember my mother making before or since.

We show love in my family mostly by doing things, by showing up: doing dishes and laundry, making dinner, buying things that need to be bought and sometimes a few that don't, putting clean sheets on beds and having cold beer in the refrigerator. I've sometimes wished we were more demonstrative, that we talked more about things other than how the towels are getting their final rinse or the dishes in the dishwasher are clean. But maybe in the end that's all there is to it: the mugs, the laundry, the things we do.

16 JUNE: ADJUSTING

I've got a weird bite on one hand, and I'm on the reference desk for another two hours, and I'm so, so tired. That is about all I say these days. I used to think I was tired sometimes before I got pregnant, but clearly I had no idea of what the word really means.

Yesterday the baby's father said that the new reality about everything is that Everyone Has to Adjust. This is true, obviously, in every possible way—I have to adjust, he has to adjust, his other children and their mothers have to adjust, whomever he's dating or I'm dating has to adjust (although I cannot imagine dating anyone again myself, not for a long, long time, if ever). That I am going to my friend's wedding this weekend seems to drive that into even starker relief. She is getting married; I am having a baby. My cousins all got husbands and wives; I get a kid. I always swore I wasn't going to be a third-generation single parent, but here I am.

Today I've had the lingering bits of a migraine all day long. An MFA grad school friend of mine used to say that she felt if she could just get Joan Didion's migraines, she wouldn't mind having them. We all worshipped Joan Didion. Presumably if you could describe migraine as well as she did, it would somehow all be more tolerable. Since I've started having migraines myself, I have come to doubt the validity of this idea. Some experiences are miserable no matter how elegantly you describe them.

I feel much the same way when researching doulas and finding out that they offer birth videography and placenta art. Well, the latter is all very well, but I can think of few things I'd less rather watch on tape than myself (or anyone else) giving birth. It strikes me as one of those sacred but deeply private experiences, the sort best remembered, if at all, only in a haze.

So I'm trying to adjust. I'm trying to adjust to feeling tired all the time, and to the idea that my body isn't mine any more, and some months from now my life won't be mine any more in the way it has been, and that I will be a single mother of an infant who will rely on me for everything. Some days I feel I can scarcely care for my cat properly. And yet I think of the two and a half years when I lived with my grandmother. They were difficult and frustrating and filled with responsibilities I'd never had before, and I frequently felt like a loser, because I was 27 and 28 and 29 years old and living, essentially, at home, and yet they were also among the better years of my life in many ways. There were rituals. There were things that needed to be done. There were groceries that had to be bought and garbage and recycling that had to be taken out. There were laundry loads that had to be carried up from the basement and others that had to be taken to the cleaners, where my grandmother had her sheets cleaned and pressed and delivered back to her in brown paper packages. There were glasses of water to fetch and television shows that came on at certain times to be watched. Many of these things, of course, were true also in my earlier solo life, but if I didn't do them, it was only I who suffered. The stinking garbage, the twice-worn socks, the dishes piled in the sink: they were my own fault, but they affected no one but me.

When I lived with my grandmother it was different. I was responsible and not only for myself. There were things to do, and I was the only one who could do them. And then, when all the other things had been done, there was the time almost every night before bed when my grandmother and my cat and I would all sit on her bed, and we'd pet the cat and talk about the present or the past or once in awhile the future. I like to think that having a baby will be a little bit like that. With diapers.

18 JUNE: STUCK IN TRAFFIC

I got up early yesterday so I could take my poor old kitty to the vet. The vet here thinks he is about eighteen and has maybe a year left to live. I've never known his actual age, and while he's clearly been ailing—lots of puking, not much eating, lots of weight lost—it's hard to believe based on his personality that he's that old. He's staying there for the weekend, and they'll test his thyroid and clean his teeth again and probably pull a few more.

Then I had to wait around for the carpet cleaners to show up, and then I packed and went over to my mother's house and waiting for her to show up (and ate some yogurt I found in her fridge—fair warning: if I come to your house, I'll probably eat everything in sight), and then finally we left for Minnesota and my oldest friend S's wedding.

Let me tell you, there's no traffic jam like one where it takes you an hour to go ten miles, and your mother has turned off the AC because she thinks the car is overheating, and you're pregnant and hungry and heartbroken. We got to the rehearsal dinner finally, at eight p.m., two hours after it started, which was fine in that it was an outdoor barbeque with live music kind of a deal, not a sit down and be served thing. R, my friend's soon to be husband, played a few of his own songs, which I love, and then he played the Townes Van Zandt song "If I Needed You," which he said was the first song he ever played for S. It nearly undid me. Knowing that Van Zandt was a heroin addict who could barely care for himself, much less his child or his partners, doesn't really even help that much—although perhaps it does. Perhaps it's good to know that you can, even in the midst of devastation, produce something so beautiful, that the sentiment is true, even if only for that moment.

And the singer's perspective echoes my own nicely: the singer is asking his beloved if. He is certain of himself, but he is uncertain of her. I'm not romantically involved with the baby's father anymore, at least not from his side, and I think that's the hardest thing I'm dealing with at the moment. My upbringing consisted of such a total disregard for heartbreak, though, that it's hard for me to know how to talk about it or experience it. My mother and grandmother, having experienced it in various forms, essentially sealed themselves off from the whole question. My grandmother was thirty-two when she and my grandfather got divorced, and she never married or even dated again. My mother was thirty-four when my father died, and although she describes her primary reaction at the time as a kind of relief—he had become intolerable, and she had planned to leave him—I think in some way she must have sealed herself off, too, though she did date again, but she never married, mostly, I think, because none of the people she liked ever liked her that much—a situation startlingly like my own.

I have not spent this much time with my mother in years. Unlike many people, I've never not wanted to talk to my family or not wanted to spend time with them, but for five years I lived 1200 miles away, and my mother doesn't really like to talk on the phone, and we saw each other only a couple of times a year. Now I talk to her every day and see her most days, and in the past few weeks we've taken two trips together. I wrote an essay a long time ago about driving my grandmother in my mother's car and about sex and about wanting to break loose in some way. I did, and now my mother drives me and her unborn grandchild around in her car, and we're all back together again, willy-nilly. In this life, you get what you get.

19 June: On Father's Day

My grandfather, who had left my grandmother many years before, killed himself when I was three months old. I never met him, though I'm told he heard my babbling, my first vowels, over the phone and carried pictures of me in his wallet till the day he died. My father killed himself when I was five and a half. I have two friends I've known long enough that they remember my father, at least a bit. One has never met her father, as her mother left him before she was born. The other has a father who barely acknowledges her and who was never married to her mother, though he has been married to a number of other people over the years.

I've never been too keen on Father's Day as a result. I pass it off as part of my eternal hatred of holidays perpetuated by the greeting card industry, but in point of fact, I have perhaps understandably mixed feelings about the whole notion of fatherhood, and precious little experience with it myself.

When I was in fourth grade, there was a girl in our school whose mother was dying of cancer. We all made cards for her, at the instruction of our teachers, and everyone was terribly solicitous toward her. It was terrible for her—I knew that even then—but at the time my primary emotion was envy. She had a parent dying and people knew about it and understood it. Her mother was dying for a reason. I thought nobody knew how my father died, and I didn't want anyone to find out. I was convinced it would simply brand me as crazy.

In years since, of course, I've come to know many good fathers—fathers of friends, and, now that I am older, friends who are fathers. They are to a man good men and good fathers, and I'm honored to have their friendship.

And I was lucky in many ways: I did not have my father for long, but for the five and a half years he was here, I had the best father a little girl could ever have wanted. He was never the dependable parent—he was famous for running out of gas, or for getting on the wrong bus, or for forgetting crucial things like my breakfast—but he was good and true in many other ways, and he loved me and he loved my friends, and he did some of the things their fathers were not there to do, giving them rides home and taking us to story time at the public library, and buying us rainbow sherbet afterwards. I always wish that everyone—my friends who grew up with single mothers and those who grew up with married parents—could have had the experience of having a father as wonderful as mine was when he was around.

But on this Father's Day I'd like to take a moment to remember absent fathers, difficult fathers, even bad fathers. We carry their genes with us, even if we don't know how or what they mean. I've been told I wash my hands the way my father did, for instance, and I know that I got his hair, and his temper. Who knows what other bits of him are lodged within me, or what bits of the fathers they never knew are lodged within my friends?

Those of us without fathers still, somewhere, had a father, and I believe we still honor that, or that we have to find some way to, because you can't, as Malcolm X once said, hate the root of the thing and not hate the thing itself. I can't, of course, actually speak for anyone else, but I cannot hate my father. He was difficult at the best of times, and of course he left me in the most final way possible. But I cannot, and do not, hate him.

And so today I remember John M. Crossett Jr., professor, printer, doubles tennis player, drinker, pipe smoker, tyrant, and, most importantly, father. Much love to you, Daddy, wherever you are.

20 JUNE: WHAT TO DO

I sent the baby's father a Father's Day card, which, as I noted to him, is the first Father's Day card I have ever sent in my life. He thanked me for it, but I think it may actually have pissed him off. It's a complicated situation, God knows, and I'm pissed off about half the time myself. I just try to avoid it, because, except in the case of political causes, I find pissed offness not to be a particularly useful emotion—and it's useful only in the kind of radical politics I do, not in actual negotiating, which I save for my day job, where that's essentially all I do.

Today I waived all but five dollars in fines for someone who recently moved out on her own after being at one of the local mental health facilities (I'm not even sure what you'd call it—it's more structured than a halfway house but less structured than the hospital) and was having some trouble getting herself together and figuring out the bus schedule. It pissed off a coworker slightly, I think, because this coworker is also in charge of overdues, and she'd already billed the woman repeatedly, and she takes that shit seriously. I really don't care, especially if we get the books back. I clearly got all my education in fines from the guys at the video store in high school who, if you pleaded with them enough, or winked, or hemmed and hawed and spun a long tale about the videos your mother was supposed to return that got buried beneath drycleaning in the back of her car, would say, "Well. . . I guess maybe I'll just charge you the tax for this," and you'd give them a quarter or something for your gigantic late fee and call it good.

I know I'm pregnant because a) I peed on a stick, b) I had an ultrasound, c) I haven't had my period since April, and d) my body is undergoing weird (though so far mostly internal) changes the like of which it has not seen before. But even though I've gained some weight, I don't yet actually physically resemble a pregnant woman, and while I know that at this stage the kid is actually slightly more than an undifferentiated blob, it's still not what I'd actually think of in any way as a baby.

The many, many pro-life billboards we saw driving to and from the wedding this weekend were, at least, free from bloody fetus pictures, but they piss me off no less than they ever have. I'm trying to decide right now if I want to do the early genetic screening or just wait till they can do amniocentesis. I'm tempted at the present moment by the latter option, because if you get a positive on the screening, they're going to recommend that anyway, and then you just have more weeks of terror and uncertainty, and quite frankly, I've had enough of that for a lifetime in the past month. (I realize, of course, that having a kid is essentially signing up for a lifetime of terror and uncertainty, but I hear there are compensating factors. I would not include morning sickness as a compensation, so I am hoping that's true.)

I went to a high school that, to some extent, mainstreamed students with disabilities. Not totally: a good chunk of the time they were still in the special ed classrooms at the far edge of the building, and by my junior and senior year I was doing nothing but honors and AP classes, and none of the special ed kids were in those, at least not during my time. But they were there, and I was always troubled, and still am, by my reaction, because my desire to believe in disability rights is in such stark contrast to my visceral, gut reaction that I would not want to live that way—and that, I know, means I won't carry to term a child with Downs syndrome, and that I'll feel terrible and mournful even though I know it would be the right decision for me.

I'm old, but I'm not that old, and so the chances remain smaller than they would be later on. It's terrifying, though: you think by the time you've decided to have the kid, you're done with the really big decisions. I suppose none is bigger than that, ultimately, but really, you've just begun.

In another month, give or take, I'll be telling people I'm pregnant—more than the few friends and the family members who already know. Then everyone gets to tell me what to do.

21 June: Grownups

Instead of doing anything else today, I've been reading through all of the archives of a blog called *When the Flames Go Up.*

That's not quite true: I finished a document I was working on that was a list of the things I've done during my first six months at work (more than I thought, especially lately, when I feel like I haven't been working at all) and a list of things I hope to do in the next six months, and I sent it off to my boss, who is leaving for a conference soon but said she'd be happy to discuss it with me when I get back. And I answered a bunch of questions from people about the cash register and I talked to some people about some other stuff and ate one meal and one snack. So, you know, not at total loss.

My friend recommended the personal blog of the mother who writes for When the Flames Go Up (which has the charming acronym of WTFGU, which sounds very much like it should stand for something else), and it looks good, but it some fundamental way I'm not quite ready to think about being a full-fledged parent yet, at least not in the "how do I get my child to sleep at night?" sense. I am, however, apparently primed to think about possibly being a coparent.

I don't know whether or how that will work, and of course I won't until the time comes. But it just dawned on me while reading this that it's possible that it might work, and that my kid might actually have two parents, in addition to its many, many family members and friends. And it was stunning, and it made me realize that my kid's life might actually be different from my life and that of my mother and uncle. It won't ever have another parent living at home with it during its early childhood, as we did, but perhaps it will have another parent around for a lot longer than any of us did. My father was gone completely after I was five. My grandfather lived until my mom was twenty-nine, but he wasn't around much at all after the divorce, when she was maybe ten, and my uncle eight. We were all of us raised by our moms, by our grandmothers, and by ourselves.

And my mother had to do everything, or find someone else she could pay to do it. She had to feed me and go to all my school things. She had to teach me to drive (something she ultimately hired someone else to do). She had to make all the decisions about where to send me to school, what I would do after school and in the evenings and the summers. My grandmother helped, of course, in that she came to stay with us a lot, but she was four hours away, not next door, or even across town.

And my mother had to live with my ongoing adoration—worship, even—of a man she had once loved but whom in the end she could not stand.

My child will have a father who will be around, who will, I think, be involved in its life in some capacity, although what exactly that will consist of isn't clear yet. It will also grow up with a mother who will have to learn to negotiate her own relationship to its father, to whom she is bound more now that she ever thought she would be during the twelve years she knew and loved him, even when he mostly didn't love her back.

My lawyer is fond of saying, "Let's be the grownups," and my family, though not in those words, has much the same idea as its guiding force. I've been lucky to grow up around people whose highest and greatest goal is always to to behave like grownups. I've been spared a lot of the crap that people I know from supposedly unbroken families have had to deal with. I hope that's something I can pass down to my kid, but I hope, too, that the kid gets to have two grownups in its life.

22 JUNE: THE BODY BETRAYS

After yesterday's almost upbeat mood, I've had a good 30 hours or so of being heavily depressed. That's almost entirely due to having done the whole "here's your stuff" "here's your house key" thing with the baby's father after work yesterday. There's a finality to that that that's worse than any feeling I know. And it doesn't help that I'm gaining weight to the point that I look chubby but not actually pregnant, and I haven't yet gotten all the gunk from my updo for the wedding out of my hair, and so it's looked for days like brown clumpy straw.

I've complained about all of that repeatedly to just about everyone I know, so I feel now like a broken record for going on about it again, but it's pretty much the only thing in my brain at the moment.

I changed my Facebook profile picture today to one that A took, because I didn't want the one the baby's father took there anymore. A friend commented that I looked happy and smiley, and then of course that made me all the sadder, because the picture was taken that same weekend, and I was happy and smiley for the same reason. Gah. I should have waited for this evening, when my mom put up wedding pictures from last weekend. I look much happier in them than I thought I would, but then I was happier at the actual wedding than I thought I would be, too.

M sent me an article this morning that I haven't finished but that is about genetic conflicts in pregnancy— basically about how the relationship between mother and embryo/fetus is not always as harmonious as one would like to think. It's miraculous, but it's also sort of parasitical, which isn't something I'd ever really thought of before. Of course, I never really thought about having a baby before at all, so this is perhaps not surprising.

The other thing I'm reading about pregnancy, bit by bit, is a book called *Making Babies: The Science of Pregnancy*, which is both informative and hilariously funny in a British sort of way. He quotes from a seventeenth century doctor named William Harvey at one point

> since the structure of the uterus, when ready to conceive, is very like the structure of the brain, why should we not suppose that the function of both is similar, and that there is ex-

cited by coitus within the uterus a something identical with, or at least analogous to, an imagination or a desire in the brain, whence comes the generation or procreation of the ovum? For the functions of both are termed "conceptions."

I have joked for years that the only way my grandmother would accept my having a baby would be for it to spring fully formed from my head, like Athena from the skull of Zeus. That may be, in the end, sort of how this has happened.

23 JUNE: THINGS THAT ARE GOOD

I'm catching up on *Mad Men*—I'm just at the beginning of the fourth season, because I am cheap and thus won't pay for Netflix (much less cable) and thus have to wait until the library gets the DVDs in. It means I miss out on all the online threads (the fourth season started what, last summer or fall?), but it allows me a faint feeling of self-righteousness. I should have asked my therapist what she thinks of self-righteousness as an emotion, since she frequently seems to disapprove of however it is that I feel. Ah well.

Anyway, today's episode started with Joan at the doctor's office finding out if all her parts were in working order to have a baby, since she had, as she told the doctor, "had a couple of procedures." Now it's my ultimate hope someday to see a character on a TV show get pregnant and decide to have an abortion, but I suppose references to a character having had an abortion are a start. And then I was thinking about how relatively few unexpected pregnancies there seem to be in the universe of *Mad Men*, given how much sex people have and how scant birth control was back then.

When I was in college I had this ongoing discussion with a good friend about which we were more scared of: pregnancy or disease. I always took the former, and she always chose the latter. I was trying to explain this to my mother, who I think was sort of mystified until I pointed out that I grew up with AIDS. AIDS and sex ed came into my life at almost exactly the same time, say around 1986, and I've never not associated condoms with preventing the transmission of HIV. People talk about how literature or music or art is all about sex and death. For those of us who grew up when I did, it's more than a matter of literature—life has been about sex and death, inextricably linked.I saw C. Everett Koop speak at the student union when I was fifteen, and my best friend and I cheered, much to the alarm of the elderly women sitting behind us, who must have assumed that we were cheering his "you're not going to tell a sexually active sixteen-year-old to Just Say No" because we were ourselves having sex, which was not even remotely the case. We just liked the sentiment. We liked anyone who acknowledged that we had opinions and that we had a right to them. We thought Koop was a hero (and, I should add, I still do).

But the things that apply when you are fifteen or twenty or even twenty-five don't apply so much by the time you're thirty-five. I suspect some old ladies will still be horrified by me. My mother said the other day that many people would just assume at my age that I went to a sperm bank. Gee, thanks, Mom. I have never, as another friend once said, wanted to choose my child's father out of a three-ring binder. But you know, whatever. People will think whatever they will think, and there's not much I can do about it but be amused.

I saw a mother with a baby at the pool today, and it occurred to me that I could someday take my baby to the pool. And that's the sort of thing that makes me happy. I get to take the kid to the pool, and to the parks I used to play in, and to the fountain downtown which, even though it's not the same fountain, is still in the same place, and is still a place that kids play. Tomorrow night I may go there with G and K and baby G, who isn't quite big enough to play in the fountain himself yet but will be soon. And next summer we'll go and he will be big enough, and maybe he'll splash some water on Baby X, who will, by then, have a name.

25 JUNE: MUSIC

I forget sometimes—though I can't imagine why or how—
just how well Bob Dylan does bitter. Better than anyone else
on the planet, really. There may be people who do political
bitterness better, but when it comes to the bitterness that one
human being can inspire in another, nobody, nobody can
beat "Positively 4th Street" (or "Idiot Wind," or "She's Your
Lover Now," or—I could go on, and on).

I'm listening to the first of those on endless repeat right
now, because it's the only thing I can really think of. I hate
being angry, but some days it beats the hell out of being sad,
and I've had enough of sad. Bitter, of course, is the combina-
tion of the two, and thus it's my overwhelming emotion toward everything right now.

Maybe when I hit that vaunted second trimester that
everyone talks about, I'll have more thoughts, or I'll write
better stuff. Right now it's all I can do to stay awake, much
less focus on anything.

Today consisted of volunteering at my CSA booth at the
Farmer's Market, napping, and watching Bruce Springsteen
videos on YouTube. Lest you think I listen to nothing but bitter music, the kid is also getting a healthy dose of the Boss
singing about the ones who have a notion deep inside that it
ain't no sin to be glad you're alive, and about getting a guitar
and learning to make it talk, and about waiting on that sunny
day. I hope it comes soon.

26 JUNE: AND THEN THERE ARE THE THINGS THAT WORK

In my complete exhaustion on Friday and my complete anger
yesterday, I completely forgot to write about the really important thing.

Friday afternoon my mom and I got to hear Baby X's
heartbeat!

It's going steady at 170 beats per minute. It is supposed to be between 160 and 180 at this stage of the game, so it is just perfect. It was truly astounding. The midwife was explaining, as she got out the stethoscope attached to the Doppler, that sometimes they can be hard to find, and you have to search, and right as she was saying that, the stethoscope landed on my abdomen and BOOM! there was a heartbeat. "Oh, you have a cooperative child!" she said. One can only hope that continues.

I could have listened to it all afternoon.

It always stuns me when something in my body works the way it's supposed to. I've had so many health problems— I have asthma, so my lungs don't work. I have depression, so my neurotransmitters are a mess. I have mitrovalve prolapse and something wrong with my back with a long name I can't ever spell, and then there were all the years of my being overweight, and there's still the way my body doesn't seem to work—I've never been able to run, or throw, or catch, even in the most rudimentary fashion.

I didn't plan to get pregnant, but clearly my body had other ideas, and for once, it decided to work perfectly. And it continues to. Everything that's supposed to be happening is happening, and the baby is doing what it's supposed to be doing, and all it seems to require of me is that I eat and sleep as much as I possibly can.

28 JUNE: WINDOWS

The goddamn internet is down here, and I don't know how to fix it. God. I'll have to get internet set up at my new place, along with everything else. What a nightmare. This is, of course, all supposing that the new place works out.

I made an offer on a house yesterday, and it was accepted today. I wrote a check for earnest money, and this may be the first time in my life I've written a $750 check and thought, "Eh, that's not that much." The inspection is on Friday, and

I'm freaking out about it. I spent much of the day freaking out about what inspector to choose. I finally reached the guy I chose while he was driving, so he pulled over to the side of the highway so we could set something up. I could never, ever manage to do a job where you have to answer your phone all the time, and where you set up appointments on the highway shoulder. I cannot imagine.

Anyway, everyone is congratulating me, and I'm convinced the house will turn out to need a new foundation, or that the electrical system will be out of whack, or that something else requiring tens of thousands of dollars of repairs will be wrong and I won't be able to buy the house after all, and I'll end up in some godforsaken condo with the general feeling that I haven't gotten anything I wanted in life. I am perhaps just a tiny bit emotional at the moment.

The lack of internet does mean that I read more pages of a book in one sitting than I have in ages, and that's to the good. I need to start losing myself more in things that are just one world—books or movies or whatever—rather than the endless rabbit hole world of online, where every new tab I open is a potential information minefield. I love that normally, but it's probably not helping me now.

The cat is napping on the sofa with me, which he's been doing a lot lately. I'd like to think this is a sign that he is getting better and that his anti-thyroid ear goop is working, but I can't even get hopeful about that. Everything just seems too dreary.

I keep thinking, "In two months I might live in a place with windows again!" and then I decide I'd better not get my hopes up. And, of course, I always worry. What if it doesn't help? What if everything is just as bad when I get there? The dishes will still pile up in the same way, and I'll still be alone at night with my computer and my cat, just the way I've always been. It never used to seem so bad, though.

My cousin had a friend who used to say, when someone had had a terrible, horrible, no good, very bad day, "So tell me the good news." Today hasn't been an Alexander day, as we call them in my family, and in fact, there's a lot of good news: my first offer on a house was accepted. I swam ten laps and felt great doing it. I actually made supper (well, sort of made—I dumped things from jars and cans into a pot and heated them, but I did chop up one vegetable, and it's more like cooking than ordering pizza). My cat is still very much among the living. As another friend of mine used to say whenever anyone asked how he was, things could always be worse. I wish that were as comforting as it always used to seem.

28 JUNE: MUSIC, AGAIN

I grew up listening to the James Taylor album *Gorilla*, listening to him singing "I Was a Fool to Care" and wishing he could be a freight train, something that keeps moving on, not remembering the past, and then listening to the song right after it, "Lighthouse," which is my very favorite James Taylor song of all time. But I listened to the album so much—dubbed from my friend's mom's LP—that the two songs have almost run together in my head, as if they're really one song, the freight train and the lighthouse, the thing that's running away and the thing you are meant to run away from.

For some reason this morning I started thinking about all this music—the music I think of as our music, my friend's and mine, because when we were kids and teenagers we were poor, and so we rarely bought duplicates of our music, when we bought at all, and didn't beg, borrow, and steal dubs from people. And we still didn't have much, so we listened to the same things over and over—James Taylor, Cris Williamson, Paul Simon's *Graceland*, Bob Marley's *Legend*, Billy Joel (give me a break—we were twelve), REM, the Pixies. Later we got on into college, and we had more money, or a little bit more, and we were much farther apart, and so we started to acquire our own copies of Ani Difranco. My tape of Elliott Smith is still dubbed from albums of hers, though, and some of her Bob Dylan started out from albums of mine.

But due to the vagaries of format and time and owner-
ship, some of that early stuff I haven't heard in years and
years. I stopped listening to Bob Marley at all sometime in
high school or college, when suddenly it seemed that everyone was listening to him, and everyone seemed to consist of
obnoxious guys who drank bad keg beer and wouldn't know
a buffalo soldier any better than Michele Bachmann knows
the location of Concord and Lexington. I loved Marley because I loved the music, but I loved the politics perhaps even
more, or I loved that it was music that had politics, which
most of the stuff I encountered in the 80s did not. My grade
school was filled with people who sang "Girls Just Wanna
Have Fun" on the way home from school. Many years later I
would write an essay about the ways in which that is a political song, but at the time I thought it was just silly. I didn't just
wanna have fun. I wanted to be smart. I wanted to do things.
I wanted to change the world.

So this morning I was streaming *Legend* in my office and
remembering times long ago, and thinking to myself that
maybe I should make sure to listen to "Three Little Birds" on
a daily basis now, just to remind myself and Baby X that every little thing really will be all right.

29 JUNE: PATIENT PATIENT

I just got an invitation to Google+ tonight. Because I am a
librarian and am friends with a lot of other librarians on the
internet and we tend to test this stuff out, I have, of course,
joined. So far it has suggested that I connect with the baby's
father. Since Gmail is always suggesting that I add him to my
emails (and when, oh when will they let me turn that "fea-
ture" off?), I'm not feeling too much love for them these
days. At least Facebook lets me hide all his posts. And he is
not, thank God, on any of my other online haunts. But the
algorithms that govern whom the world thinks you should be
connected to are, apparently, primitive. That may be to the

good. Would it feel better if some Googlebot suggested removing your ex from your contacts after "reading" your break up email?

Almost all I think about though, these days, is food. Unless I've just eaten, I'm usually thinking about when I will eat next and what I have that I can eat, preferably quickly. The latter part has led me through two and a half large containers of cottage cheese in the past three days. "I didn't even know you ate cottage cheese!" my grandmother said. "Trust me," I said, "neither did I." It's been going in phases. For awhile all I wanted was macaroni and cheese. Now it's all about burritos (and, apparently, cottage cheese). Yogurt is a constant, and toast is often good. Things that are too dry or require much in the way of chewing are generally out, which makes keeping snacks in my office to munch on hard. Chocolate still sounds horrible, although other sweet things aren't quite as bad as they once were.

Sadly, I have almost no desire to eat all the interesting and exotic things provided by my CSA. Under normal circumstances, I'd be thrilled about learning to make nettle soup, or experiment with bok choi, or come up with new uses for kale. Right now, though, it all sounds like way too much work. Boiling pasta often seems like too much work these days. I don't have time to cook: I need to eat NOW. And more. And again!

At the hospital last week they said I'd gained four pounds. I feel like I've gained about twenty. One is, of course, supposed to gain weight during pregnancy—I'm just always shocked that, given the way I eat, I haven't gained more. I try on clothes in the morning and am half horrified by how dumpy I look (thank you, o conditioning of Western culture) and half amazed that anything still fits at all. I keep thinking the day that I tell everyone I'm pregnant everything will suddenly be a lot easier, like I'll have excuses for being hungry and exhausted, and I'll get to let my belly hang out all I want.

I have to get up early to go see my psychiatrist. She's seeing me once a month for the duration of the pregnancy and postpartum period, which is probably good, although it does make my life feel like an endless round of medical appointments—therapist and midwife last week; shrink this week; therapist again next week; new primary care doctor the week after that. But if there's one thing I'm good at, it's being a patient. My patience itself has been rather tested of late, but I'm managing.

30 JUNE: TOO TIRED

to write anything tonight.

Tomorrow I will maybe write about Paul. Or not. Home inspection in the morning; haircut in the afternoon. I am remaking my life. Or at least my hair and living arrangements. I hope.

1 JULY: THE GREEKS VS. THE CHRISTIANS

Today I had a home inspection and learned that something about Home and Auto Maintenance class in high school paid off: the wiring in the basement that I thought was dangerous is, in fact, dangerous. Of course, I think anyone who looked at it would think that.

Then I got my hair cut, which always feels good, even if it's not an exciting or spectacular haircut, which it's not.

Other than that I just napped and ate today, since tomorrow I have to work.

Last week's Old Testament lesson was Abraham and Isaac, and the sermon was all about trying to convince us that it was not an awful and barbaric story. Since I've never thought of it as an awful and barbaric story, I did not pay much attention, and instead, as is my wont, started thinking about other things. But now I've been thinking about the story again, and how it's really a story about God asking something from you and, when you agree to give it up, giving it back. That's a rather common story trope, actually, except that it works out much better for Abraham and Isaac than it does for, say, Orpheus and Eurydice—because of course Orpheus ultimately can't really give Eurydice up, because he doesn't trust or believe in the gods enough, and so he loses her.

Christianity is, in that sense, a great deal more comforting than the religion of the Greeks, because things do come back to you, and people come back from the dead, and life is restored, and God provides, and the loaves and fishes multiply, and Sarah has a child in her old age, and it's all good. Nothing like this ever happens in Greek mythology. There's lots of satisfying revenge, but no real blessings.

Of course, I've always liked the Greeks, and possibly for just that reason, because that's how life has always seemed to me—that mostly good things don't happen, and even when you get revenge, it's just as cruel as it is sweet. I've always found those things to be comforting. I've always liked tragedy as a more accurate representation of life than anything else.

I still think that a lot of the time, but I also think possibly there's a point to believing in redemption.

3 JULY: SEEING STARS

After many days of nothing much happening aside from my being sad and then happy and then scared, today was kind of a doozy.

I got up early to go to church, because I was reading at the early (7:45 a.m.!) service, and my mother was preaching. I got there, and I read the incredibly long lesson from Genesis and led everyone in the bit from the Song of Solomon and made it through the very convoluted bit of Paul just fine. And then Mom did an excellent sermon about Rebekah being a person who, despite how it sounds, actually does have agency, and then we did the old version of the Nicene Creed, with all things visible and invisible, and the quick and the dead, and I did the intercessions, and we confessed our sins against God and our neighbor, and we passed the peace, and we got to the Eucharist. And by the time that came around, I was feeling rather tired, and thinking that perhaps right after communion I would sneak out and go lie down on the sofa. And then I went up to the rail and got my bread and took a sip of wine, and I was kneeling and desperately hoping the person next to me would hurry up and get her sip of wine so I could go, and—

The next thing I remember I was lying on the ground, and Dr. H and some other man were telling me to wake up, and I wondered why they were in my house trying to get me out of bed, and then they said no, you're in church, and I thought, "well, church must be over, but it's still odd that they're waking me up," and then I heard people murmuring about the body and blood of our Lord Jesus Christ, and I realized that church was actually still going on, and that I had fainted right in the middle of it.

They got me out to the sofa—the blessed sofa!—and had me lie down with my feet above my head, and then suddenly there were EMTs, and they were asking me if I had a history of seizures, and it came out that my mother thought I might have had a seizure (my mother, who did not think my hives were an allergic reaction to penicillin!), but Dr. H thought not, but then everyone seemed to think we ought to be sure, and then the ambulance was there and I was off to the hospital, where I spent the next couple of hours getting an IV of water and having my blood pressure taken by a machine every ten minutes or so and getting an EKG and feeling terribly embarrassed because really, all I did was faint.

They let me out eventually, and C picked me up—my mother was still back at church preaching at the second service—and I came home and passed out for awhile, and then my mother and the people whose house I've been staying in, just recently home from England, came home and there was a flurry of activity, and my mother brought me an omelet, and later we went to the mall to get new phones for some of us, and I am mostly feeling better. I think that means I'm just normal tired instead of fainting tired. Small favors.

I texted the baby's father from the hospital about the whole thing. In a smaller and meaner moment I was tempted not to tell him about it at all. We wrote back and forth a little, and he checked in this afternoon to see how I was doing. He's also been commenting on my Facebook posts, which makes me both more and less inclined to post there. I just keep plodding along, one day at a time.

Right now the fireworks are going off in Iowa City, down by the river, but I'm too tired to go and watch them, so I'm just listening and imagining. I'm going to stop typing now, and stop playing with my new iPhone, and go to bed, and hope that tomorrow (a day off! finally!) is a little less exciting.

4 JULY: HEY BABY

The best part of today—well, aside from a lovely long nap and having someone else buy groceries and make dinner—was that I got to play with Mr. 2.5, the baby's father's son, whom I adore, and who even remembered me, saying my name over and over as soon as I arrived, in that endearing way that small children have where it sounds as though there's a W instead of an R in the middle of the name. I wasn't at all sure he'd even remember who I was. The baby's father had finally noticed, or remembered, or something, that there were more things of mine at his house, so I'd gone over to pick them up, but I stayed because Mr. 2.5 seemed so glad to see me, maybe even as glad as I was to see him.

I'm continuing to read, slowly, this book on the science of pregnancy, which is mostly making me realize that we know even less about women's health than I thought we did—and I didn't think we knew much. Of course no one knows what exactly causes morning sickness, although I was interested to learn that one theory is that one of the hormones released by the placenta is structurally similar to thyroid suppressing hormone, and so they think it might muck up your thyroid. "Well," I said to the kitty, "perhaps we both have thyroid problems!" He is doing much, much better on his new medicine, but I don't think I'll try it. And the nausea part is mostly over—just the fatigue remains.

I almost wish I could take part of my leave now, just so I could sleep half of every day.

A friend of mine posted an old music video of Dave Alvin singing "4th of July" to Google+ today, which made me nostalgic for being a Big Wooden Radio groupie way way back in the day when they used to play downtown every summer. That and listening to the NPR people read the Declaration of Independence are the sole markers of my 4th of July celebration this year, which is just fine with me. I always used to throw a gigantic anti-4th-of-July party for all my activist friends. Ten years ago it got busted. Eleven years ago— the very first one—was the summer I was living on Brown Street and driving the baby's father's 1983 Subaru, much to the confusion of many people. "So how is it you have his car?" people would say, and I would say, "It's a long story."

I imagine I will be saying that now for the rest of my life. "How is it you have this kid?" "It's a long story." A much, much longer story now, but one that will, I hope, have a better ending.

5 JULY: ABOUT ME

I am astounded, truly stunned, by how much I eat. Today, for instance, went something like this:

- yogurt
- 2 pieces of toast
- cheese and tomato sandwich
- grapes

- noodle thing from a box (glorified ramen, really — it claims to be two servings, to which I say HA)
- yogurt
- bagel with cream cheese
- 2 large tortillas with beans, chicken, veggies, and salsa
- 3 large glasses of apple juice
- nectarine
- raspberry sherbet

And now I'm sitting here thinking I'd better eat some cheese and possibly something else before I go to bed, because my stomach is growling again.

I've been eating like this for a month, and I've only gained five pounds. I feel like I do nothing but eat. (And yes, some cheese and some cranberry juice seem to be in order. I'll be right back.)

Ah. Better. Although of course by the time I wake up, I'll be starving again. This baby, according to something I read, is now the size of a small lemon, but it's got an appetite like me at camp, when I used to make triple-decker peanut butter and jelly sandwiches for dinner, and eat several of them. And a big bowl of yogurt. And a big bowl of tabouli. And some fruit. And anything else I could get my hands on. God, that all sounds good.

I had more energy this morning than I've had in a long, long time—since before I got pregnant, I think, or before I knew I was, at any rate. I woke up in the morning without hitting snooze. I made and ate breakfast and even made my own coffee. I did some real work at work this morning. It didn't last all day—by the time I got back to work after my second housing inspection, I was ready to do not so much for the rest of the day. But I didn't have that desperate need to lie down on my floor and sleep, and that was a great relief, too.

In an attempt to try to repeat that wonder now, though, I'm going to go to bed again.

7 JULY: TIME AND MATERIALS

You know you're pregnant when the meditative flow yoga class makes you break out in a sweat and get out of breath.

Honestly. There I am, breathing deeply, thinking about all this right/left masculine/feminine energy balance the teacher is talking about, attempting to move smoothly and gracefully through the very mellow series of postures, and suddenly in the midst of triangle I realize I'm sweating and breathing heavily. Ridiculous.

On the other hand, I made it to yoga, which hasn't happened lately, and I did make it through. The teacher just ran across the entire state of Iowa and was trying to pump everyone up for this special class this weekend that, so far as I can tell, involves doing yoga on a tightrope. But you know, whatever. I just do my thing and hang out in down dog and contemplate how my belly now pretty much touches my thighs every time I bend over, and not because I'm that flexible.

I read an article today about pregnant women being denied mortgages because, you know, they are obviously going to be on maternity leave and not earning money and then they'll probably just quit their jobs and not have an income, so you can't loan them money. I made a note to wear my skinniest-looking outfit when I go meet with the mortgage broker. Mind you, I haven't quite figured out how I'm going to take any maternity leave and pay my bills, but I figure more will be revealed.

I'm convinced I look pregnant now. Of course, I've often had this conviction before. When I was twenty-three and waiting for the bus one day, a man even asked me when my baby was due. I'm fairly sure that it's basically impossible to grow up female in this society and have any remotely realistic notion of what your body looks like, so I mostly try not to think about it. I succeed in this about as well as I succeed in ignoring the heat and humidity of summer in the Midwest.

I'm half looking forward to just getting over with telling everyone I'm pregnant, because then I can stop worrying about looking pregnant, and because I assume everyone online will say nice things, and God knows I love an online ego boost. But I dread it about equally, because of course I'm terrified that people will ask questions I don't want to answer, or will say judgmental things I don't want to hear. I spend an enormous amount of psychic energy steeling myself against shit that people say. I always figure that keeps me from getting hurt the way I see some of my friends getting hurt, but I'm not really sure—I may spend as much effort on my armor as they do on their recovery. And sometimes the armor doesn't work, and then you're out the energy twice over.

I haven't cried in four days. That seems like a fairly major miracle.

I'm praying now for another day of good energy. Tuesday was good, and today was good. Wednesday was almost as bad as the worst days of last month, and I had to lie down on my office floor for fifteen minutes once again just to save myself from having to hold myself upright for awhile.

The next thing I need to get up the energy to do is to email my editor and say I just can't do the theatre column any more. I keep putting it off, and of course that will just make it worse. But I don't even go to the theatre these days, and writing it just makes me feel like an imposter. And I need all the time I can get for myself.

9 JULY: CONVERSATION

From earlier this evening, by telephone. At my mom's house, my mom and me. At my grandmother's house, my grandmother, my cousin M, and his wife A.

> Gran: Don't you have something you want to tell M? About your *house*?

> M: Yes, I hear you are nearly done?

Me: Indeed I am. Right now I am, at my realtor's advice, giving the seller a few days to get nervous that I'm about to walk away from their latest counter remedy offer.

[Details of housebuying and discussion of the great merits of realtors and other experts. A joins us on the phone.]

G: M and A have some news, too. A?

A: No, I want M to tell it.

M: Well, we are expecting a baby in January.

Me: Wow! Um. You are never going to believe this, but so am I!

[The next minute or so of congratulations is drowned largely by squealing.]

M: Yeah, we have just started telling the family. My dad was like, "Congratulations. Now let me tell you about my new bathroom tile."

Me: OMG I THINK HE IS RELATED TO MY MOM.

[Laughter]

Their baby is due five days after mine. A and I both just started feeling better this week, although we were both tired today. My grandmother is over the moon with excitement that she gets to have two great-grandchildren. M and A and I are all excited that our kids will have each other as cousins. It's all so much family happiness it nearly makes you sick. I love them, though. M is four years younger than I am and is the brother I never had, even if he did once vote for a Libertarian.

12 JULY: NAMES

I've never been able to read *Lolita*. I keep trying, because I know Nabokov is a wonderful writer (I loved *Speak, Memory*, even though of course I think they were all on the wrong side of the Russian Revolution). But I can't get more than a paragraph into his masterpiece. Most people who can't read the book have issues with the whole pedophilia aspect. I have an issue because, I'm told, my father actually suggested Lolita as one of two possible names for my half-sister.

I fared somewhat better in the name department: my father, having informed my mother that he would choose a girl's name, since she had chosen a boy's name, presented her, sometime after I was born, with a list of three names on a piece of paper: Cordelia, Elizabeth, and Laura, and told her she could choose whichever ones she liked. I've been grateful for my whole life that she rejected Cordelia immediately, and so I became Laura Elizabeth by default.

The story with my half-sister is that my father and his first wife couldn't agree on a name. They'd already had a boy, and they just named him after my father and grandfather, but the girl left them floundering. Finally my father said he was reading two books named after their female protagonists. He'd just tell V the names of the books and she could choose one. The two books? *Pamela* and *Lolita*. My father's first wife, I'm told, knew just enough about literature to know that she didn't want to name her daughter Lolita. I'm not sure that Pamela is a great fate, either, but nobody has read *Pamela*— well, nobody without a PhD or a bizarre fondness for epistolary novels, and even they probably don't immediately associate the name with the book.

I have named several cats—Skia and Samuel, and I contributed to the name of my mother's cat Bean. I also name all my cars (the Octopus, the Sphinx, the Phoenix, Sally, Viktor—yes, I've had kind of a lot of cars) and several bicycles and one viola. I like naming things. I hope I do a good job with the one coming up.

15 July: Narration

I'm quite sure I'm not actually having a baby.

I woke up this morning and for several minutes thought about the day and then thought, "Oh, I'm pregnant" followed immediately by, "That can't be right." I mean, it is becoming more apparent on a daily basis. Few of my clothes fit anymore. I ordered one of those bands you can wear around your midriff to cover up unbuttoned pants, and it's arrived. I have an appointment in another couple of weeks to have a giant needle stuck into my uterus, and I've seen the kid moving around on the ultrasound. But it still just doesn't seem real. Someday, surely, I'll wake up from this fantasy world and find I'm just back in seventh grade doing geography homework and figuring I'll have a boyfriend when I get to college.

And yet I find myself resting my hand on my belly all the time. I don't notice it, and then I notice and am slightly baffled—have I suddenly become obsessed with having a potbelly, like Bruce Willis's girlfriend in *Pulp Fiction*? Have I adopted some weird new posture in my mid-thirties? I can't figure it out. But then I find myself like that and think well, I guess that's where the baby is, and so I say hi, baby. Hope you're doing okay. What did you think of lunch? V makes a pretty mean chicken salad, doesn't she? It's the grapes and dried cranberries that do it really, I think. Of course, some raw onion would really have kicked that whole sandwich up a notch, but I can't complain too much. Sorry we haven't been swimming lately. The pool here's closed, and I never seem to make it over to any of the other pools, and now that the month's half over it seems dumb to spend money on a monthly pass at the U. Maybe next month?

I always figured if I had a kid I'd be one of those people who read poetry to it in utero, or played it all of the organ works of Bach or something. But no, instead I natter, and try not to get too upset.

24 JULY: JUST WAITING

Last weekend I was at the Ministries School and Retreat that my mother runs. Sadly, I was there neither to study nor to retreat but rather to take pictures of the event and make a video of them. I also decided it would be the test run weekend for telling people I was pregnant. That went reasonably well. Everyone seemed pleased about the pregnancy. Of course, half of them thought I was a college student. "What are you majoring in?" they'd say. "Uh, well, fifteen years ago I studied Greek," I'd say. "I'm 35." Of course, that doesn't preclude being a college student, so then I'd say, "No, actually I have two masters degrees and a full-time job." Our rector seemed pleased largely because it would mean an unbroken six year string of pregnancies at our church. "We don't do a lot of marriages," he said, "but we do a lot of baptisms." Well. I try to help out. Only one person asked about the father, and she didn't ask who he was, just if there was a father involved. So that was good.

So church knows, and my family knows, and some friends know, and that leaves… everybody else. And that's the part I'm kind of dreading. Work will be weird. And telling the friends I haven't let in yet will be particularly hard, since they're the most likely to ask questions I don't really want to answer. Or perhaps it will all be fine, or not as bad as I think, but it's gotten me back to a point where I often wish I could just hide under a rock and let someone else run around like the town crier announcing to all and sundry.

I wonder if everyone who's pregnant feels this way?

I had coffee with the baby's father this afternoon and then he worked on my car for a bit—I ran into the edge of the garage the other day and the front bumper is a bit loose again. I sort of hate to accept help, but I'm trying to remember that it's something I'm going to have to start doing, and from a lot of people.

I also have an actual essay brewing in my head. We'll see where that goes.

Two and a half weeks till I move into my new house. The day cannot come soon enough.

28 JULY: AMNIOCENTESIS

Today I took my elderly cat to the vet to have his thyroid checked. The vet decided they wanted to run some other blood screens, too (what do we care for expense?), so as he was having blood drawn, I said to him, "Samuel, I had a much larger needle stuck into me yesterday." Then I explained to the vet that I had had amniocentesis. I'm always amused at how freaked out male vets seem to get when I discuss human female medical problems or procedures. My old cat once had a yeast infection in her ear. The young male vet was explaining to me that there is a delicate balance between yeast and bacteria in some areas of the body and sometimes it got out of whack. I said, "Oh yes, I'm familiar with that problem." He turned beet red. I am terrible.

But anyway, I did indeed have a large needle stuck into me yesterday, and I owe a great debt to my friend K for taking me to the appointment and for the baby's father for saying a prayer for us before hand. On the whole, though, it's an anti-climatic sort of a thing. They spend a lot of time doing the ultrasound and measuring things.

Nurse: That's an arm.

Inner Laura: Um, okay, whatever. Looks like a white blur to me.

Outer Laura: Oh, neat! Hi, kid's arm!

Then you get all painted up with betadine, and then they pick a spot, and then they pull out some fluid. It's like getting blood drawn only more elaborate and with a lot of people in the room.

Everyone also always says, when looking at ultrasounds, "Look at the little alien!" It struck me yesterday that we've got that backwards. We have no idea what aliens look like, but apparently we've decided they look like fetuses. What exactly that says about the human race I shan't ponder now. In the meantime, though, I can report that the blob now looks very much like a fetus, which in turn, it seems, looks like an alien.

9 AUGUST: NAMES, AGAIN

I've been calling the baby Baby X because it amuses me, but it did dawn on me early on that it was also appropriate as the name of at least one of its chromosomes.

Yesterday I got the call from the hospital: no chromosomal abnormalities, no spina bifida, no any other things that are bad. And a Y chromosome.

So. I am having a healthy baby boy. This freaks me out a bit (boys! boys are mean! they always got to the marbles first in preschool, and they never shared!), but as usual I've been too busy with work stuff and traveling (more on that later) and today with moving that I've barely digested it. But the good amniocentesis results do mean that I will very shortly be making a public internet announcement. These have been the most difficult and strange—but, I hope, ultimately rewarding—months I have ever been through.

I'm not sure I can recommend moving 1200 miles, starting a new job, getting pregnant, and buying a house all in the course of nine months (and the nine month figure is not lost on me), but here I am, and here I go.

10 AUGUST: MOVING

So yesterday I moved to my new house. It's amazing what you forget to mention when you've got chromosomes on your mind. And today I told the internet I was pregnant. They were unsurprisingly pleased. And everyone at work paraded into my office with a baby book bag.

And last weekend the baby's father and I went down to visit A and her family in Missouri.

My friends all thought this was crazy, and I suppose it was. It was crazy of course because really, who goes on a trip the weekend before they move? But it was crazy mostly because, really, who goes on a trip with their ex-boyfriend who is the father of their unborn child whom until recently they were barely speaking to and whom they are still not dating and probably won't be and. . . well, yes. It was very strange.

It happened because the baby's father and I had begun talking again, tentatively, mostly by text. I would get texts from him—nice texts, not crazy ones—and so I would respond, and he would respond again. This was in late July, maybe, and I was preoccupied with the approach of August 6, and with the idea of being pregnant and back in the town where my father died on the thirtieth anniversary of his death. I give perhaps too much credence to days, to anniversaries, to the passage of time, and yet last year was the first time in decades that the date didn't bother me. I was afraid that this time it would.

And so the baby's father contacted A down in Missouri to see if we could visit that weekend, and then he told me we were set to go.

Are you sure? I texted back. He was.

Saturday he and A's husband and their friend went flying, and A took me shopping for maternity clothes, which I desperately needed. That night people came over for dinner, and I wore one of my new dresses, and everyone drank toasts and read poems, and A and the baby's father got into this intense discussion of people they'd known in graduate school, at which point I suggested to everyone else that we ought to talk about something they knew nothing about, and they apologized sheepishly. And it was good. Much, much better than being by myself would have been. I think eventually maybe happy memories can outweigh sad ones. But you have to build up a lot of them.

26 OCTOBER: UP AND DOWN

Today is one of those days when I am seemingly overwhelmingly sad. I miss my father so much, and I am so sad that like me, my baby will only have one grandparent, because all the rest of them are dead. Then I remember that actually the other three grandparents I had died after I was born—my maternal grandfather when I was three months old—I never met him—my paternal grandfather just months before my father, and Ethel, his wife, some years later. I got to know the two best of my grandparents—Poppa, my father's father, albeit too briefly, and my mother's mother, who is still with us and whom I went to visit last weekend. So like me, the baby will have one grandparent and one great-grandparent, which is, I suppose, more than a lot of people have. But it saddens me still.

This weekend my grandmother made reference to "my married granddaughter-in-law." I'm sure it was unintentional. I know she doesn't really care that I'm not married—except that of course at some level she does, and probably at some level I do, too, or it wouldn't bother me so much. It's hard to figure out if that's societal conditioning to the idea that you're supposed to be married to have a kid or if it's some more inborn desire to have a partner in the undertaking. As I said to someone a few weeks ago, I don't have a partner: instead, I have a guy who mows my lawn, is doing tilework in my kitchen, asks how I'm doing, and sometimes brings me dinner. In other words, it's exactly like having a partner, only minus the parts that people usually think of as making up such a relationship. I could be much worse off. But that doesn't make it easy.

This morning after I take a shower and stop crying I'm going to the animal shelter to look for a new cat or two. My wonderful old cat Samuel died last week—I had to put him down, actually—and while I want to have an appropriate mourning period, the house is much too sad with just me in it. It needs feline greeters. The allergists and the OMG you can't change kitty litter while you're pregnant people can be damned. I think of the kitty litter thing as something for people with no other worries to worry about. They're the sort of people most pregnancy books seem to be written for, and I suppose probably they don't really exist, but God, the mere idea of them is annoying. Of course if you're pregnant you must be in a committed heterosexual relationship and looking forward to decorating your nursery in pink or blue! It's like 1952 in pregnancy books, only with organic baby food and no BPA.

I was originally going to write every day of my pregnancy, or as close as possible. Obviously that hasn't happened, as it's been ages since my last entry. But I'm glad it's still here, particularly as a record of those first months. I am officially in my third trimester now, and the baby moves constantly, as he has since he started (finally!) at twenty-three weeks. Well, of course, he was moving before that, but not that I could feel. Now it's like a constant party. I'm never sure if I'm invited or not.

The baby's father said the other day that he could see the baby was being very active. We were at the local Occupation, where he was participating in a reading of "Howl." It's bizarre—I can't see it at all—I suppose the angle is wrong—but I guess other people can, at least if they are looking. I hope they aren't all looking. It seems very private, having your baby move. It's why I haven't posted ultrasound pictures anywhere but on this blog. For some reason I don't really want everyone in the world looking at pictures of the inside of my body and my unborn child, nor do I really want to give those pictures to Facebook. It's complicated, because I've always lived a fairly public life, but suddenly I feel that somehow my child shouldn't be forced into that. I want to write more about the experience, but I'm never sure if someday the baby won't grow up and be horrified that the world could read about him before he was even born, or that they know the details of my doubts about having him. It doesn't seem fair to a kid for the world to know that, although at the same time it doesn't seem fair in some larger sense not to acknowledge the truth that babies aren't all conceived with joyful intent and longing, that some of them "appear overnight, as mushrooms do," and yet are no less loved.

21 NOVEMBER: CHILDBIRTH EDUCATION

I wanted to take the fancy mindful birthing class at my yoga place. I haven't been to my yoga place in months, which may explain why I somehow missed the announcements for the class, which started back in mid-October. It also cost $300, which means it's probably just as well I missed the whole thing. Instead, I've registered for a childbirth education class at the hospital where I'll be giving birth. It cost $60, which is still annoying but not probably totally unwise.

The class meets in a basement level room in the oldest part of the hospital. They send you elaborate directions on how to get there—park in this ramp, take this elevator, turn here, go through these doors. It's the part of the hospital I once knew best—after all, I grew up here—but it's changed, and I got lost. Or rather, perhaps I didn't get lost, I just thought I was, because the doors that led to the hall that led to the room we were supposed to be in were locked, and a couple and I had to bang on them to get someone to come let us in.

I had expected this class to be sort of awful, but I hadn't imagined it would be quite as awful as it was. I was the only single mother—the one other single person there turned out to have a husband who couldn't come. Everyone seemed young and svelte and prosperous, although I'm sure that wasn't actually true. The yoga place class would theoretically be *all* people like that, since a) it's yoga and b) it's spendy. But feeling like the black sheep wasn't the worst part. The worst part was the class itself.

For an hour and a half a nurse read to us from canned PowerPoint slides with embedded video clips. We all got a booklet with a special access code that would allow us to watch these video clips from the comfort of our own homes for three months. The booklet had couples of all different skin colors, but they were all heterosexual. And all couples. Still, all this would have been tolerable were it not for the content. For the first hour or so, we were all told we should eat lots of vegetables and drink lots of water during our pregnancies. We should avoid soft cheeses and processed meats and various kinds of fish. We were told that we should only need an extra two to three hundred calories a day and were handily provided with clip art examples of where those extra two to three hundred calories might come from ("half a turkey sandwich and a glass of skim milk!").

I looked around thinking, this is a class full of people who are all having babies in January and February. Isn't it a bit late to be telling us what we ought to avoid, especially during our first trimester?

Then began what I suppose was the real meat of the class. The nurse informed us that there were four Ps to childbirth: passenger, passageway, powers, and psyche. She kept pronouncing the last word *psych*. I kept thinking, I am making Thanksgiving dinner for somewhere between seven and ten people in three days and I don't have a turkey yet. I used my psych and got out of there, grabbing one of the free bottles of water (next to the free bottles of Sprite and the salty and sugary snacks) on the way out.

25 November: Buy Nothing Day

I am not sure what compelled me to feel I should host Thanksgiving dinner for an indeterminate number of people at my new house while seven months pregnant. I invited my grandmother, who stayed at my house for a week, my mother and our friend L who is living at her house at the moment, my friend C and any of her children who could make it and her partner if he wanted to come, and the baby's father and any of his children who could make it. None of them could—their mothers all wanted them. My mother invited a friend of hers. I had very little idea who all was coming until they showed up that day.

Considering all of that, things went quite well. C and her Mr. 5 showed up around noon, and my mother's friend not too long after, which was good, as Mr. 5 requires a certain amount of, shall we say, supervision. My mother came mid-afternoon, the baby's father around five, and C's partner and our friend L just before dinner at six. Other than a complete meltdown by Mr. 5 just before we were going to eat, everything was great, and other people put away all the food and did all the dishes while I lounged on the sofa. I figured this was the first and last time I'd get away with such indolence, and I'd better take advantage of it.

My family is a tight-knit bunch—the family motto is, we say, "We find ourselves preferable." My great uncle had it put into Latin and printed up and hung in his house, but he always told visitors that it defied translation, perhaps out of a desire not to seem obnoxious, although more likely out of a desire simply to be enigmatic, which was his style. But despite that members of my family have been welcoming people into our homes and to our dinner tables for years. My grandmother and grandfather shared a home for a year or so with his stepsister after her husband died, and their children grew up together, so much so that even long after my grandparents were divorced, that family became a part of ours. I still enjoy rattling off the relationships. "Oh, we will have

Christmas with my mother's father's stepsister's daughter and her family," I'll say.

When I was little, after my father died, we had a series of live-in sitters. My mother would offer room and board to a college student in exchange for them being around in the evenings and at night on nights she was on call. She was in medical school, so there were a lot of those. A carpenter who installed some wood floors in our house became such a good friend that when he told my mother he owed her some work, she sent him to live at my grandmother's house for a week and fix things there. He invited all of us to his wedding. For a time when I was in high school and college, my mother's ex-boyfriend lived at our house, and now our friend L lives there.

I draw a distinction of some sort between family and not-family in my mind, still, but when it comes to the dinner table, all are welcome.

I try to convey this to the baby's father, that he is welcome, that we are thankful for his presence, however much of it he may want to give. And he has been coming around, at least—coming over to fix things in my house, accepting dinner or a cup of coffee, playing endlessly with Mr. 5 when everyone else was exhausted by him and I was finishing dinner. Everyone has seen his goodness; I hope only that he can see it in himself.

ADVENT

4 DECEMBER: MARY

The Bible is full of women who become accidentally pregnant. Lacking sticks to pee on, they instead have angels to deliver the frightening news. Well. The angels are frightening. In most cases, the news is welcome, since the women are frequently old and considered barren. The exception is Mary, who if not frightened is at least initially startled, being as how she's a virgin and all. That fades, though, fairly quickly, and next thing you know she's busting out with the Magnificat.

Now that it's Advent, the Magnificat shows up at pretty much every church service. I had never given it much thought before this year. But last week, on the first Sunday of Advent, I sat there in my pew and thought, "Oh yeah, Mary! She was an unwed teenager with an unexpected pregnancy! Perhaps I should pay attention!").

Unfortunately, the account of Luke leaves you with little to go with if you are looking for reassurance, or at least for sympathy. Granted, Luke is an economical writer and also most likely a guy, and thus his narrative focuses mostly on the bare bones. Angels show up, Elizabeth and Mary get pregnant, and voila, nine months later they give birth. You do get the nice scene between the two of them when Mary shows up to tell Elizabeth she's going to have a baby, and Elizabeth's baby, at six months in utero, jumps in the womb for joy. That part seems like an actual pregnancy. But one can't be blamed for wanting a bit more. Did either of them have morning sickness? What was it like for Mary to be traveling right before her due date, in the winter? Do you get to complain about back pain or labor if you are carrying the savior of the world?

One also wonders about what everyone around her thought. It's true she was carrying the son of God, but did other people believe that? Jesus was met with a certain amount of doubt during his lifetime; one imagines his mother must have had to endure something similar. Did people really believe she was carrying the son of God, or were they actually running around muttering about how she and Joseph must have been fooling around before their wedding day? "Yeah, that's the son of God you're carrying, and I'm the Queen of Sheba." (Did Sheba even exist then? Well, it doesn't now and people still say that, so I guess it hardly matters.)

Early on in my pregnancy my mother told me that I was old enough and well-to-do enough that I could just figure everyone would assume I'd gone to a sperm bank. I was horrified. How in God's name was that better? I dislike lying on principle, even by omission, and I couldn't believe that anyone would go around thinking I'd chosen my baby's father from a three-ring binder. Or an online profile. Plenty of people do this, of course, and I have no objections to it, if that's what you want, but why would someone like me, who'd never even planned to become pregnant or ever thought she wanted a child go such a route?

I have no idea what people assume. Maybe they figure I went to a sperm bank. Maybe they think I got drunk. Maybe they think I was in some sort of terrible abusive relationship. The truth is none of these things and is, in the manner of truth as Buddy defined it to Zooey, rarely pure and never simple. Someday I will have to figure out how to explain it to my son. I owe him that much. But the rest of the world— well, as I see it, in that regard, I owe them nothing.

20 DECEMBER: O CHRISTMAS TREE

In December 1982, a year and a half after my father died, and just around the time of my seventh birthday, I was at the grocery store with my mother one day (oddly enough, the same grocery store I now shop at), and she asked me to choose a Christmas ornament from a display. The one I chose still lives somewhere in wrapping paper in the ornaments she hasn't unpacked in years, the ornaments I'll inherit at some point. It's a large sphere with a cream colored background and a sleighing scene around it, and at the top it says, "A Father's love brightens the season."

I'm not positive about the capitalization—I haven't seen the thing in years—but I'm pretty sure that's what it is. I think it's even in Papyrus, or some precursor to that now overused typeface. But maybe it's simply what I need it to be, because I need it to be the heavenly Father, and not my own father, who had not brightened any season at all in a whole cycle of them. I cannot imagine what my mother thought, or what she thought all the years of my childhood as I reverentially unpacked the ornaments and hung that one in a place of honor.

I'm thinking of it now because I'm looking at my own tree, currently mostly barren of ornaments, but strewn with lights. It's the first real tree of my own I've ever had. Even though I've lived away from home for many years, I never had a tree because I could never be bothered with it, and because I figured I was leaving town for Christmas anyway, and because, well, it always seemed like so much work. But yesterday evening the baby's father got a tree and brought it over and set it up for me, and then took me to buy lights for it, and now it sits illuminated. I took a photo of it with my phone and sent it to him just now, and then I remembered he sent me a photo of his tree after he got it up a week or so ago, and then I thought how odd it is that we're sitting four blocks away texting each other pictures of our respective trees.

I was for some reason discussing this whole tree issue with my therapist the other day, and she said, "Well don't get one this year, because next year you'll have to have one because you'll have kid."

"Dude," I said, "the kid will be eleven months old. He won't have the foggiest idea of what Christmas is or what a tree is. He's not going to care at that age."

"Hmm. I guess you're right," she said, and we moved on to other things.

But I suppose I did want a tree this year because it somehow signifies that this is our home, that I am invested enough in this place to buy lights and store ornaments from year to year. Tonight I also set up the olive wood creche set that my mother gave me. It's right by the tree, and Mary and Joseph and the angel and the shepherd and some cattle and sheep are already there. The wise men and their camel are on top of one bookshelf, and they'll slowly make their way toward the scene till they arrive at Epiphany. I couldn't figure out what to do with the Baby Jesus until Christmas, so I put him in my jewelry box. It still seems rather cruel, keeping him away from everyone. Surely someone has made a creche with a pregnant Mary and then a postpartum Mary with the baby Jesus? But for now he will have to wait separately as his earthly parents wait for his arrival, as I wait for the arrival of my own son.

God is, I suppose, the ultimate absent father. What do we say when we pray to him, after all? *Our father, who art in heaven.* He isn't even in this earthly realm. When he does show up, it's always in enigmatic forms, and often they are frightening. Who wants a father in the shape of a burning bush? Jesus must have had a strange childhood, knowing Joseph was his father for all intents and purposes here on earth, but that he wasn't really his father, and that his real father was, for the moment, unreachable. *O God, O God, why hast thou forsaken me?* If you're looking for someone looking for a father, look no further.

And yet of course we know as well that God is love, that he sent us his only son, that he is omniscient, omnipotent, and that his love is not for a season but for all time.

I believe that about my father's love, despite his absence, and about the baby's father's love, despite his. Surely Joseph loved Jesus as his own, and surely we all do the best we can.

31 December: New Year's Eve

There are worse feelings in the world than that of knowing that the person you love doesn't love you, but when you're in the throes of it, it's hard to remember what those worse feelings are.

On this, the last night of 2011, it seems that the baby's father and I are both in the throes of that particular emotion, in classic love triangle fashion. I love him, he loves his ex, and his ex—well, God only knows what she feels or thinks. I've never met her. I just know she's "in a band" and that she doesn't seem to see much of their son.

I try to avoid writing about all this, because it's an invitation to a pity party, and it's not really fair to the other people involved. But I'd be lying if I said it didn't weigh on my mind.

I was born to parents who should probably never have gotten together. I was, as some people think, spared from my parents' divorce, although I'm not sure that having your father die really qualifies as a better outcome. It puts you in a peculiar sort of position, fitting in not quite with the other children of divorce but also not with the much smaller group of children with a dead parent, either. You can't talk about shuttling between your parents, but neither can you mourn with those whose parents had happy marriages that ended in tragedy.

And how do I even begin to categorize my son, or to explain to him, when the time comes, how his parents came together and why they no longer are? I can only hope the answer becomes clearer to me by the time he is old enough to see other families and to ask questions about his own.

I was born at near the end of the calendar year and my son will be born near the beginning, but I will always think of him in terms not of the secular calendar but of the liturgical one: conceived at Easter, decided on before Pentecost, born sometime after the baptism of Jesus. I have watched the church year especially closely this past year, thinking as each season turns of the strange thing that is happening to me.

It is New Year's Eve of the calendar year as I write this now, and soon I am going to bed, and when I wake up, I'll have to remember to write a new year on my checks. Other people in my town will be out and about past midnight. The last time I did that was a week ago, on Christmas Eve, when I went to midnight mass at our church. I drove downtown through empty streets, past darkened stores. All the pizza joints and liquor stores were closed, and even most of the gas stations. No undergraduates were out on the sidewalks, underdressed for the winter weather. No police cars patrolled the streets. It is a rarity nowadays, in most places in this country, for anything to be closed. For almost everything to be closed all at once feels almost as if the world has become holy. Certainly that was my hope on Christmas Eve. I came home and put the baby Jesus in his cradle in the manger of the creche, and then I went to bed. Tonight marks a new year for some, but for the Wise Men, it is just another day on their journey, their cold coming. I will move them a few steps farther before I go to bed tonight.

2 JANUARY 2012: FREEBIES

Yesterday afternoon, while my mother was making hoppin' john and cornbread and then running out to get white rice because her hippie daughter only has brown and she thought that was not traditional (though we've never eaten hoppin' john and cornbread on New Year's Day before, and it was, my southern friends would tell me, Yankee cornbread, most decidedly not the real thing, and I made garlicky lacinato kale, not traditional collard greens to go with it, so I'm not sure just what tradition here we were breaking), it suddenly dawned on me that I needed a changing table.

I had been thinking that I would just use the top of the small dresser in what will eventually be the nursery. It's the right height, it has drawers, it's there—it seemed perfect. But of course the drawers have baby clothes in them, and the top doesn't have any kind of railing to keep the baby from rolling off, and also my mother will need the dresser as a nightstand when she's staying with me after the baby is born, and—well, suddenly it seemed imperative to get a changing table, stat.

I hopped on Craigslist, did a little search, sent an email to a guy in North Liberty, heard back from him two hours later, called him, and secured for myself a freebie. Today I borrowed the baby's father's old car and went to pick it up.

The guy and his wife live in this town to the north of my city in a new subdivision where all the streets are named for animals, many of which never lived here and most of which don't live here now. Black Bear Bend. Timberwolf Road. Grizzly Trail. There's a Billy Collins poem somewhere about how names like "Pheasant Ridge" are actually elegaic, memorials to the animals that were displaced when the people moved in. I like to act high and mighty about how I used to live in a place where large animals still existed, but of course they've been shoved aside in Wyoming, too. The bison get chased back into the park whenever they leave. The elk all get directed to a winter feeding ground in Jackson, where they spend the winter eating food we give them and contracting brucellosis, which they then either do or do not pass on to domestic cattle, depending on whom you believe. The black bears and grizzlies and wolves, especially, can't be herded and are thus protected by laws, but their territories are still blocked by roads and houses and all the other things we humans have set in place.

I was at one point making a list, to amuse myself, of restaurants in Wyoming without dead animal heads on the walls. It was a very short list.

These were the thoughts that ran through my head as I went to get this changing table, which seems quite sturdy and which was, of course, free, my favorite kind of thing. "I'm done," the wife said as she called her husband out from the bowels of the basement. "I am not having any more kids." I almost told her that I wasn't planning to have any, and that I hoped her plan for being done included her husband getting a vasectomy, but I refrained. The people on Craigslist don't need to hear my life story.

I went on a date once via Craigslist, in Chicago, in the early days of Craigslist when it was confined to major cities. I was 27 or 28, and I think I just wanted to see what it was like. It turned out to be like drinking a lot of beer in some Hyde Park bar with a graduate student in a subject I no longer remember. He had a roommate who had a cat named Rosa. "Is she named for Rosa Luxembourg?" I asked, and the roommate was thrilled. You can never go wrong by guessing that cats owned by left-wing University of Chicago graduate students are named for old Communists. That cut short my online dating career: I remember the cat, and my conversation with the roommate, but not the guy's name.

I officially hit 37 weeks this past weekend. That means the baby could show up any time in the next five weeks. He continues to move and kick, although he's clearly frustrated by how little room there is left for him to do anything. There are four days left of Christmas, and I move the Wise Men now every night, along with their camel. They are waiting, too.

5 JANUARY: DOWNTOWN

The city I lived in has banned panhandling downtown, at least in theory, although as I walked through today I saw there were still several people at their posts. I am rarely downtown nowadays, though, and so I see the panhandlers who have been driven out from downtown, or who never liked it anyway, who now station themselves at crossroads at the outskirts of town. I pass two of them every day on my way to and from work. I am never sure how lucrative their positions are. They are visible and in high traffic areas, so their cardboard signs that say HOMELESS WITH KIDS are seen by many. But the high traffic also makes them hard to get to. There are multiple lanes, and lots of cars, and getting to the right side of the road and not holding up traffic and fiddling around to find cash in your wallet—all these things take time that commuters may not have. I never seem to.

I am sitting now in the swanky coffee shop above the independent bookstore in my town. I used to sit here years ago and try to write, and today for some reason I felt compelled to try again. I have the afternoon off today because I work again this evening, and the electricians are working at my house, which makes hanging out there unappealing. So I came downtown, to the places I used to go.

I've been avoiding downtown for months. Partly it's that I'm seldom called upon to come here. The yoga studio I like is downtown, but I have been too tired to do yoga. The public library is here also, but I rarely come to do anything but pick up and drop off books there. But I've been avoiding it also, I know, because I am pregnant. I'm not sure what I am afraid of, except of some sense that I will here run into not just someone I know, but into my former self. Walking through the coffee shop today, I got just that feeling. The barista was discussing his thesis footnotes with another patron. People were bent over books and papers at their tables. Two young women looked at me with something like shock as I carried my cup of coffee, my belly leading my way. This is not a place where pregnant people hang out.

I am just shy of two weeks of my due date. Unlike many women, I have a fairly exact notion of when this baby was conceived, but that of course does not mean he will actually appear when the midwives say he should. The online week-by-week pregnancy calendar I've been following talked a week or two ago about how your baby's movements might start to feel... different. The language of pregnancy is full of such inexactitudes. The baby's first movements feel like frogs, or like giggles, or like—like something no one can quite define. "How do you know it's the baby and not just indigestion?" a friend asked when I finally began to feel him move. "I just do," I said. And I did. And I couldn't think of how to explain it either—not what it felt like, not how I knew. I just did.

Those earliest movements are different from the kicks that come later, and indeed, in this past week, I have felt something different yet again. I describe it to people by saying that I think the baby is frustrated—he's so big now there isn't as much room for him to move—but now instead of kicking or paddling or turning somersaults his movements feel more like seismic shifts, like a sudden rippling under the water of a still pond, or a mole hill sped up from time-lapse photography, or a bubble of lava rising from the earth. Sometimes it's just a tiny piece that rises, a heel or an elbow. Sometimes, though, the whole baby shifts inside you, as if your belly were actually a wave and your baby a body surfer riding it. He wants something, he wants out, but he's not quite ready yet.

EPIPHANY

16 JANUARY : MARTIN LUTHER KING JR. DAY

My cousins beat me to it. Their baby was born yesterday, 36 minutes after they arrived at the hospital, ten days ahead of his due date (which, it should be noted, was five days after my due date). Benjamin Michael weighed seven pounds, two ounces, measured nineteen inches long, and was born, according to my mother's notes, with "much hair." I have yet to see a picture, but he's undoubtedly cuter than my baby will be. My mother said, "Well, he will always be older, but Peter will be bigger for a long time. Of course, eventually Benjamin will be taller." So reassuring. I assume that my baby will be two weeks late and involve 26 hours of hard labor.

I am beginning to think my mother is more excited about the family bassinet than she is about the baby. She brought it over, in pieces, yesterday. She has been talking for weeks about the custom mattress she ordered for it, which arrived in the mail today. "Your grandmother will be pleased by any pictures we send of the baby," she told me awhile ago, "but especially by pictures of him in the family bassinet."

A few days later, she started talking about how she probably needed to find the skirt for it ("you remember that, right?"), as my grandmother might not feel the picture was complete without it. Well, no, no, I don't remember. The only time I ever saw the thing is when I was a baby. For the past thirty-six years it has been sitting around gathering dust, or holding stuffed animals, or, more recently, yarn. That one's offspring is more desirable if pictured in a dressed up spindly family heirloom is a bit hard to get used to.

I am going to encourage my coworkers to start a pool betting on my delivery date. At least then when I walk into work I'll feel that their disappointment in seeing me there is monetary rather than personal. I know, of course, that they aren't really disappointed to see me. I guess this last bit of waiting takes forever for everyone.

Epilogue

29 January: On this rock

Peter Malcolm Keene Crossett was born one week ago, on Sunday, January 22 at 6:49 p.m., after 36 hours of labor and a little assistance from a vacuum extractor. He weighed seven pounds ten ounces and was twenty inches long. He came out and started waving his arms within seconds, just the same way he'd moved them in the womb. And just as they said in the books, my pain level went from unbearable to barely there within minutes of his birth, and after they checked him over I was able to hold him, sweat and tears and joy running down my face.

It's possible we went a little overboard in naming him. His father and I actually realized a couple of days after he was born that we really should have given him an L name, too, so he could be Peter MLK Crossett. My mother was totally horrified and explained that we couldn't change it because none of the L names we thought of scanned well. She finds it hysterical that this was the argument that won us over. I told her we weren't really serious about doing it; we just liked the idea.

We were in the hospital for an extra day because Pete's temperature kept dropping, and they thought he might have an infection and thus put him on antibiotics for a day. Nothing seemed to show up, though, and so they sprung us from the joint on the 25th, at which point we were very happy to go home and get some rest. At the hospital, they have a board in your room in the Mother/Baby Unit with the name of your current nurse, your doctor or midwife, and various instructions and information. The instructions said "Rest and Enjoy Baby!" followed by "take 4 baths a day" and "walk in halls 3-4 times a day" and yet more instructions about paperwork to fill out and I forget what all else. And then people keep coming in to talk to you or take your blood or your temperature or your vital signs. On the second day, people started coming in at 7 a.m. and did not stop until 1:30 p.m., at which point one of the nurses offered to put a do not disturb sign on the door. I have never been so grateful for anything in my life. My mother was off at her office or something, and so Peter's father and Peter and I all just sat quietly for awhile and then drifted off to sleep.

Peter is astonishingly beautiful and astonishingly mellow. He has lots of dark black hair and dark, dark blue eyes, the color of the sky just before night falls, or the lake in Maine in certain lights, or some gemstone that has yet to be discovered but that would be my very favorite. He waves his arms as if he's conducting a symphony, and his hands are like little starfish, fingers spread wide and waving slightly. He looks at everything, and he grimaces and smiles, and in his sleep he looks just like his father when he is sleeping.

I'm not sure if I ever wrote about how terrified I was that I wouldn't love him, that he would be one of those ugly, scrunchy babies, that he would cry all the time, and most of all that he would have no personality, that he would just be a small machine that ate and peed and pooped. I can't quite believe I ever thought such things now. He is a full human being and was from the moment he was born. And being with him is even better than being alone.

I just finished Lauren Slater's book *Love Works Like This*, in which she theorizes, among other things, that women who have a history of mental illness and who have to stay on medication during pregnancy and who have psychologically difficult pregnancies actually may be at less risk of postpartum depression, not more, because in some way they have already worked through all the difficulties, whereas mothers for whom the whole pregnancy is a period of joyful expectation have not. It's only been a week, and of course I have no idea if this will prove to be true, but I feel already like a different

mehow that doesn't matter: I get up and
rs and his insatiable appetite and his cry-
him, and I know at long last that we both

person. Looking at what I've written o
months is astounding—I can't quite belie
was, how awful so much of it was, how in
thing seemed.

Last night the baby's father and I we
mark the thirteenth anniversary of the day
back together or anything, but, well—it
strange journey, and it seemed somehow
the date. I have known him now for more
life. We went to the same pub that we al
although we ordered a lot more food and
used to because I am not nearly as poor as
birth was announced to the departmen
teaches the other day, and I would kill to
the wall in the faculty lounge, th

person. Looking at what I've written over the past eight months is astounding—I can't quite believe now how sad I was, how awful so much of it was, how impossible the whole thing seemed.

Last night the baby's father and I went out to dinner to mark the thirteenth anniversary of the day we met. We're not back together or anything, but, well—it has been a long strange journey, and it seemed somehow important to mark the date. I have known him now for more than a third of my life. We went to the same pub that we always used to go to, although we ordered a lot more food and drink than we ever used to because I am not nearly as poor as I was then. Peter's birth was announced to the department where his father teaches the other day, and I would kill to have been a fly on the wall in the faculty lounge this past week—this must be the best gossip fodder they've had in years. His father says the younger faculty members have all been kind but also that a few of the older faculty have checked in warmly, all of the people who knew one or the other of my parents. Someday I will take Peter to the English building here and tell him that in addition to his father, his mother, his grandmother, and his grandfather all once worked there in some capacity or other. Peter will never meet my father, of course, not in this world, but that there are people who still remember him is a blessing to us both. Surely as long as someone remembers you you are not really dead, and the more people who remember, the more parts of you are alive.

I'm sitting and typing this while Peter naps. There is sunlight streaming in the windows of the house I bought for us. My mother is at church and Peter's father is driving to Mount Vernon to pick up Mr. 3, and later today they will come over and we will have a party to celebrate Peter's one-week birthday (Mr. 3 loves birthdays). It's not that I haven't cried, or gotten frustrated, or scared, since Peter was born. There are plenty of times when I look at him and think, where did you come from? And why are you here? And do I really have to get up right now? Can't you just wait another hour or so? But somehow that doesn't matter: I get up and deal with his diapers and his insatiable appetite and his crying, and I look at him, and I know at long last that we both belong here.

ACKNOWLEDGEMENTS

Many years ago I heard the director Alan Pakula give a commencement address. Why, he asked, don't cars come with lists of credits the way movies do? "Windshield wipers installation by so and so. Steering wheel mounting by thus and such." I've said all along that this baby ought to come with a list of acknowledgements. This, then, is a list for both the baby and the book.

Thanks to my early readers, supporters, and dear friends: Marianne Reddin Aldrich, Greg Bales, the Rev. Sara Quigley Brown, Jenna Freedman, Martha Hardy, Iris Jastram, Steve Lawson, Kathy Lyons, Rachel Erekson McKinney, Catherine Pellegrino, Caitrin Rames, and Margaret Smith.

Thanks to Jenna for proofreading and suggesting subject headings and to Walt Crawford for *The Librarian's Guide to Micropublishing*, which I used in formatting and copyfitting this book. Whatever errors remain—and I'm sure there are many—are my own fault, but there would have been many more without their guidance. Thank you to Steve for designing the cover.

Thank you to Kathy and Catherine and my coworkers Beth Bartlett and Ellen Hampe for their willingness to have endless discussions of the vicissitudes of pregnancy. Thanks to Jen Sherer and Ryan Downing for their friendship and for the hand-me-downs, and to Ryan for installing the car seat in my tiny car. Thank you to Carol and Larry Hunsicker for giving me a place to live in the first months I was back from Iowa, for saving so many clothes from their grandchildren, and above all for their many years of friendship and support. Meg White should have lived to see both the baby and the book. I owe her both thanks and apologies.

I did not know Aliki Barnstone until just a month before the story of this book began, but she, Craig Cones, and

Zoë Barnstone-Clark have since welcomed me to their home and their hearts.

The staff at the Women's Health Center at the University of Iowa Hospitals and Clinics are to be commended for their excellent care and for their kindness. I thank especially Laura Dellos and Jennifer Steines-Wagemester for taking so much time early on in my pregnancy to answer questions and just to sit with me, and all the nurse-midwives—Laura, Elizabeth Cook, Elizabeth Potter, and Lynne Himmelreich—for their care throughout my pregnancy. Melissa Mitchell, my doula, provided guidance and companionship throughout my labor, and I couldn't have done it without her. Thanks as well to Ellen Smith for long-distance question-answering. Dr. Barbara Brown and Jeanne Melick-Shield were crucial in taking care of my brain and my mind.

I am grateful to the people of Meeteetse, Wyoming and to my many Wyoming friends for the five wonderful years I spent there before moving back to Iowa and to an adventure that may yet rival my time in the West. I am grateful to the people of Trinity Episcopal Church in Iowa City for continuing to welcome me back time after time.

AskMoxie.org, the pregnancy calendar at AlphaMom.com, and many of the posts tagged pregnancy at AskMetafilter were great reading while I was pregnant. *Our Bodies, Ourselves: Pregnancy and Childbirth* and *Ina May's Guide to Childbirth* were the best books I read on the actual subject. Anne Lamott's work, especially her early novels *Hard Laughter* and *All New People*, as well as the indispensable *Operating Instructions* helped keep me sane in the very worst times.

Above all, though, I would not have survived without the support and love of my family—the Crossetts, the Wallaces, the Hillmers, the Serafins, the Inskeeps, and all the rest—I love you all more than I can say, and I am grateful every day to be blessed by their presence in my life. My grandmother, who shares this book's dedication, lived just long enough to see it in manuscript, though not to read it all. Though I am sure she would have disagreed with much of what I have portrayed here, I hope that, in the end, she knows it was written with both truth and care. I thank the Rev. Cynthia Bourgeault and Lucy King for welcoming my son into their extended family. To Nate, Georgia, Thomas, and Hart—you all have your own stories, just as important as this one, but not mine to tell. My love and thanks to you all.

Many stories begin *in medias res*, perhaps because it is so impossible to know for sure when a story really begins. Part of my story begins on the January day in 1999 when I met Tom Simmons, but that is another story for another book. In the meantime, I thank you, Tom, for reading this difficult manuscript and above all for your presence in my life and in Peter's.

Peter's story truly begins with the day that Tom brought Aliki Barnstone and Robert Pinsky to Iowa as the headline acts for World Book Day. I hope that Peter's life will be influenced by their grace and talent, just as his beginning was.

Lastly, I thank all my friends in the computer—the Library Society of the World, the denizens of FriendFeed, and others too numerous to name but no less dear. The web—and the world—are better places because of you.